FROM PECKSNIFF TO THE PRINCE OF WALES

Charles Knevitt is a journalist, author and broadcaster, and has been Architecture Correspondent of *The Times* since 1984.

Born in America in 1952, of British parents, he was educated at Stonyhurst and the University of Manchester, School of Architecture. He has contributed to all the leading architectural and building publications and occasionally to magazines abroad. In 1987 he wrote and presented Granada Television's award-winning documentary, 'Rebuilding the Region', in its New North series.

He is the author or editor of nine books including *Space on Earth*, a companion to the six-part Anglia Television series for Channel Four on which he was consultant; *Monstrous Carbuncles; Community Architecture* (with Nick Wates) which is being published in a Japanese edition this year; and the best-selling *One's Life*, a cartoon biography of The Prince of Wales.

He collects cartoons as a hobby.

THE MODERN ÆSOP

PVNCH VOL XX

LONDON:
PUBLISHED AT THE OFFICE 85, FLEET STREET.
AND SOLD BY ALL BOOKSELLERS.
1851.

From **PECKSNIFF** to the **PRINCE OF WALES**

150 Years of Punch on Architecture, Planning & Development
1841-1991

Charles Knevitt

Foreword by Lord St John of Fawsley

POLYMATH PUBLISHING
Streatley-on-Thames

'The brazen plate upon the door (which being Mr Pecksniff's, could not lie) bore this inscription, "PECKSNIFF, ARCHITECT", to which Mr Pecksniff, on his cards of business, added, "AND LAND SURVEYOR". In one sense, and only one, he may be said to have been a Land Surveyor on a pretty large scale, as an extensive prospect lay stretched out before the windows of his house. Of his architectural doings, nothing was clearly known, except that he had never designed or built anything; but it was generally understood that his knowledge of the science was almost awful in its profundity.'

Martin Chuzzlewit by Charles Dickens, 1843–44

'My chief object has been to try and create discussion about the design of the built environment; to rekindle an alert awareness of our surroundings; inspire a desire to observe; but, most of all, to challenge the fashionable theories of a professional establishment which has made the layman feel he has no legitimate opinions.'

A Vision of Britain by HRH The Prince of Wales, 1989

For Lesley

The author would like to thank the following for their contributions to *From Pecksniff to The Prince of Wales*: Peter Morgan, picture researcher; Anne Cowlin, my secretary; Lesley Harvey, photocopyist extraordinaire; John Taylor; Sara Drake; Paula Chesterman (formerly of *Punch*); Amanda-Jane Doran and Miranda Taylor in the *Punch* library; and Lord St John of Fawsley for contributing the Foreword. Last, but by no means least, my thanks to Donaldsons, Chartered Surveyors, and particularly to Ray Stenning, the partner responsible for the project; and to Sally Greenway and Sheji Brettle of The Quentin Bell Organisation.

From Pecksniff to The Prince of Wales is sponsored by:

DONALDSONS
Chartered Surveyors

Published by Polymath Ltd,
The Old School House,
Streatley Hill, Streatley-on-Thames,
Berkshire RG8 9RD, England.
Telephone: 0491 875032   Fax: 0491 875035

First published 1990
Selection and text copyright
© Polymath Ltd, 1990
Cartoons copyright © Punch Publications Ltd, 1990

ISBN 1 873224 01 X
Designed by Chrissie Charlton & Company
Typeset by Nene Phototypesetters Ltd, Northampton
Printed and bound in Great Britain by
The Southampton Book Company, Southampton.

CONTENTS

THE BATTLE OF THE STREETS.

WHILE the battle of the gauges is dividing the railway world, the battle of the streets—the contest between the broad and the narrow—is revolutionising the metropolis. Unfortunately for the narrow, the broad carries, or rather knocks down, everything before it. We shall soon be utterly without a lane or an alley throughout the whole of London; while as to architecture, the old brick and tile order will be utterly superseded by the modern stuccoite. It is all very well to enlarge the streets if we can enlarge the means of the people sufficiently to enable them to live in them; but if the habitations of the poor are superseded by palaces, while pauperism still remains, we would simply ask what on earth is to become of it.

The old police principle of "move on," "you can't stop here," seems to be now generally applied to those of humble means, and the question is, "Where are they all to go to?" So as they are got rid of somehow, this is a question which gives little trouble to those who are bent on "improving" a neighbourhood.

1845

ANTI-UGLIES

Some highlights of architecture

THAT Angry Young Architect, WRIGHT,
built a skyscraper six miles in height.
  Then he got on the blower
  to MIES VAN DER ROHE
and sneered: "Is the Summit in sight?"

Sighed JOHN NASH to DECIMUS BURTON
"Fashions change, but of one thing I'm certain:
  Our classical terraces
  will be treated as heresies
e'er the stucco's had time to get dirt on."

With top hat and cigar, what a swell
was ISAMBARD KINGDOM BRUNEL.
  Having laid the Great Western
  regardless he pressed on
and launched the Great Eastern as well.

"To save our Cathedrals," said WYATT,
"there's nothing I won't have a try at;
  from Durham to Sarum
  no horrors I'll spare 'em.
'Ruat tectum, justitia fiat'."

That sober Tractarian, FERREY,
spent an evening with TITE and got merry.
  Next morning the squinches
  were out by three inches
while the spire looked decidedly jerry.

The churches of J. SOMERS CLARK
fell (æsthetically) wide of the mark.
  In fact LEONARD STOKES,
  making one of his jokes,
said "They look at their best after dark."

"Let it rain, let it snow," chuckled GOLDIE,
"*I* don't care if the brick's going mouldy.
  Let the smoggy air smirch
  every bit of my church
then the experts will think it's an 'oldie.'"

"By GEORGE," cried Sir ERNEST to PETO,
as he tore off a strip of sgraffito,
  "I like EYCK, and your Flemish
  seems quite without blemish.
Now Gothic's a style that I veto."

The stately old Duke did a slow burn
when the last guest departed from Woburn.
  "Still, 'e's took quite a bit," coughed
  the butler to FLITCROFT,
"and 'e 'adn't no Zoo back in Holborn."

Said STUART to NICKY REVETT
"How classically Greek can we get?"
  "Our columns 'in antis'
  should please dilettantes—
and also they'll keep out the wet."

"Why, man," chortled TREADWELL to MARTIN,
"dig this crazy new style that I'm startin';
  it's a real cool art-nouveau
  that's right in the groove! Oh
how RUSKIN—that square—will be smartin'."

P. E. C.

1959

FOREWORD

Edmund Burke, that great Whig writer and political philosopher of the eighteenth century, maintained that there were Three Estates in Parliament, 'but in the Reporters' Gallery yonder, there sat a Fourth Estate more important far than them all' (Thomas Carlyle, 1841).

To which, I think, should now be added the Fifth Estate: Cartoonists. For as Charles Knevitt wrote in one of his previous cartoon anthologies, 'Cartoonists have always been among the most perceptive social commentators of their day, as well as persuasive campaigners for a better world. With a few strokes of the pen and still fewer well-chosen words they can convey what it might take a leader writer a score of carefully composed paragraphs to get across with infinitely less precision and wit.'

Punch has always enjoyed a special place in my affections, not only for its humorous content but also for its reforming zeal over the past 150 years. In my role as chairman of the Royal Fine Art Commission for the past five years, I welcome especially this collection of more than 250 cartoons on architecture, planning and development drawn from its archives.

In the following pages we can see the glories of the past, such as St Paul's and the Crystal Palace, as well as some of the monuments to Mammon which today are recognised for what they truly are – travesties of architecture, the greatest of the arts. Each year the Commission receives about 300 schemes upon which to comment and although it formally comments on only about half of these, I should like to think that its influence has increased dramatically in recent years as the built environment has become, quite rightly, a matter of great public – as well as professional – concern.

By taking a satirical look at what has been built by preceding generations, this memorable collection of cartoons will not only help us to laugh at our – and other people's – mistakes, but will hopefully guide us to a better future. It is, quintessentially, an English view, and, as Jim Schoff has written, 'The English sense of humour is no fragile flower, blooming exotically in some hot-house. It is, rather, a hardy perennial which clings tenaciously to the sharp edges of life like bindweed on a bomb site.'

I hope that as many people as possible will have an opportunity to enjoy this book, compiled by one who has established himself as one of our most brilliant architectural critics.

Preston Capes, Northamptonshire
August 1990

St John Fawsley

Lord St John of Fawsley

THE STABLE.

Landlord. "YES, MR. PUNCH. NICE, CLEAN, AIRY BOXES, PLENTY OF LIGHT, PERFECT DRAINAGE AND VENTILATION. THE BEST OF FOOD AND WATER, AND KIND TREATMENT. THAT'S MY PLAN!"

THE COTTAGE.

MR. PUNCH (TO LANDLORD). "YOUR STABLE ARRANGEMENTS ARE EXCELLENT! SUPPOSE YOU TRY SOMETHING OF THE SORT HERE! EH?"

1861

MR PUNCH'S VISION OF BRITAIN, 1841–1991

Punch, or the London Charivari was born on 17 July 1841, four years after Queen Victoria came to the throne. In that same year Joseph Whitworth invented the street-cleaning machine; handling a football joined the rule book at Rugby School; Hong Kong was acquired by Britain; and Barry's Reform Club opened in Pall Mall. Mr Punch was the eponymous editor, a mythical, grotesque hump-backed figure with a leery eye and hook nose, based on the Punch and Judy puppet-show character, Italian in origin, and dating from almost two centuries earlier.

The 'guffawgraph' and 'refuge of destitute wit' was, at first, a champion of the poor and oppressed, lampooning the people, events, social conditions and vagaries of progress which marked the day. Soon, however, it began to reflect the more self-satisfied concerns of its increasingly wealthy, and middle-class readership. What began as an irreverent chronicle of its time became, in the space of 30 years, a national institution.

Amidst its well-deployed armoury of essays, jokes and criticism, its graphic journalism – the cartoon – is the most pungent. In 1843 the magazine inadvertently coined the modern use for the term when a competition was held for tapestries to hang in the rebuilt Palace of Westminster. 'Punch decided to produce its own entries and these were political,' wrote R G G Price. 'The success of the series made the paper continue it and the term "cartoon" gradually became attached to any picture of a politico-satirical kind' – and latterly to describe any humorous drawing.

From its very earliest days, Punch joined the Quarterly Review, Blackwood's Magazine and The Spectator in moulding Victorian ideas on architecture, planning and development, rivalled only by the Illustrated London News and The Builder, both launched in 1842.

There was no shortage of targets, whether from an aesthetic, political, social or economic standpoint. During the magazine's first 20 years Britain was reaching its zenith: it was responsible for 25 per cent of the world's commerce and 40 per cent of trade in manufactured goods. It consumed just under half of the raw cotton output of the globe, produced half its coal and lignite and more than half of the world's iron. More than a third of the world's merchant fleet flew under a British flag. All this from a country with just two per cent of the world's population, and 10 per cent of that of Europe.

But dramatic growth brought with it all the problems of rapid – and muddled – urbanisation: satirists joined the social reformers in campaigning for clean water, better housing (stables of the wealthy were often a vast improvement on the cottages of the poor) and the repeal of the window tax. Medieval lanes and alleyways were demolished to make way for the railways and broad avenues of palaces, leading to what *Punch* depicted in 1845 as 'The Battle of the Streets'. Overcrowding and displacement were rife, not only in London but industrial cities such as Liverpool, where there were still densities of 1,200 persons to the acre in 1884.

Redevelopment of cramped housing areas led *The Builder* to comment, in 1851:

> Who builds? Who builds? Alas, ye poor!
> If London day by day 'improves',
> Where shall ye find a friendly door,
> When every day a home removes?

Punch also railed against contemporary aesthetic taste and judgement, suggesting in 1846 that the new arch at Hyde Park Corner became an 'advertising station', 'which will have the double advantage of covering up an eyesore [a statue of Wellington] and turning it into a source of profit'; decrying how Nelson's Column (erected 1842) had sacrificed ornament to use, and showing it as a 'melancholy ruin' discovered by archaeologists in the year AD 2346; and mocking the design for the new east front to Buckingham Palace which, it decided, should house shops at street level, so that 'the Royal children might be allowed to acquire a practical familiarity with the retail commerce of the country', thus promoting 'affability in the Royal children, and loyalty among the subjects of our gracious Sovereign'. The 'nation of shopkeepers' should know no social barriers!

While at times facetious, *Punch* shared with its Victorian readership a general loathing for the previous generation of great builders – the Georgians. They considered buildings of the period 'dull, monotonous and uniform', according to Professor Asa Briggs, who quoted J S Morritt, a contemporary gentleman of taste, criticising 'long rows of shops and houses ... tortured into strict uniformity, exactly of the same height, with the same thin slices of pilasters, the same little flourishes of ornament'.

But as well as reflecting these criticisms, the magazine could not resist also attacking what followed: The Battle of the Styles, not least in street and railway architecture. Individual houses could be dressed up as pantomime groups or symbolic of their owners (a steam-engine, strong box or bull). Meanwhile, 'on the great lines of Railway one may fancy one's self traversing all the countries in the world within half-an-hour, for he is very likely to encounter an Old English ticket-office, a Turkish water-tank, a Swiss engine-house, a Grecian goods depot, and an Italian terminus, all within the limits of fifteen miles of railway'!

WORK FOR THE NEW GRAND MASTER.

BROTHER PUNCH (*loq.*). "NOW THAT YOUR ROYAL HIGHNESS IS HEAD MASON, I HOPE YOU'LL DO YOUR BEST TO IMPROVE OUR PUBLIC ARCHITECTURE; AND, ABOVE ALL, THE DWELLINGS OF THE POOR."

1875

Potential President of the Royal Academy. "AND HERE, AUNTIE, WE GET THE SIDE ELEVATION."
Auntie. "HOW DELIGHTFULLY THOROUGH! I'D NO IDEA THAT ARCHITECTS DID THE SIDES AS WELL."

1919

When the style was not quite so eclectic, it tended to settle on Classical or Renaissance for public buildings, and Gothic for churches, thanks largely to the architect Augustus Welby Northmore Pugin's books, *Contrasts* (1836) and *The True Principles of Pointed or Christian Architecture* (1841). And with the possible exception of St Thomas (the 'doubting' Thomas of the scriptures), who is the patron saint of architects, it is the Pugin family who came to epitomise the architectural profession and, it transpires, provided the role model for Pecksniff.

Seth Pecksniff, the architect, land surveyor and humbug of Charles Dickens's novel, *Martin Chuzzlewit*, was thought at the time of publication to be a caricature of Samuel Carter Hall, editor of *Art Journal*. More recently it is believed that Dickens based him on a conflation of A W N Pugin and his father, Augustus Charles Pugin, with Hall. Status and training were the two key issues of concern to the rising professions of the building and development industry, and Dickens elaborates on both. As a pupil in Pecksniff's office, Martin Chuzzlewit comes up with his own design of a school, rows with his master, departs for America, and returns to find his design being built – but Pecksniff taking all the credit!

The younger Pugin's 'contrasts' of ancient and modern architecture – very like those employed by Leon Krier, the Prince of Wales's master-planner of a model development at Poundbury Farm outside Dorchester – betrayed his High Tory origins: with others of the Gothic Revival he was against capitalism and its built manifestations, the secular factory chimneys replacing the religious towers and spires of medieval times. But both Dickens and *Punch* believed in the concept of 'progress', scorned the Pugin/Pecksniffs and the widespread corruption in the industry, and looked forward to better days.

The single most important event – and building – soon arrived and it epitomised the 'Spirit of the Age': the Great Exhibition – and the Crystal Palace, so named by the magazine – of 1851. Prince Albert, the Queen's consort who championed the show, was earlier taunted by *Punch* over his lack of employment (echoed in the early 1980s by newspaper comment on Prince Charles) and was initially hostile towards his brainchild. It even illustrated a spoof architect's design for the building, modelled on the Prince's famous hat, which he fashioned himself.

But it then changed its editorial tune and rallied to the cause of showing off the technological advances of the first half of the century. Beneath 19 acres of glazing, in a building three times the length of St Paul's, there were 14,000 exhibitors who drew six million visitors – well over twice the then population of London. It was a huge popular success.

For *Punch*, the Crystal Palace embodied all the virtues it found so lacking in either classicism (in 1845 it described the Parthenon as being of the exact same colour and mouldiness as a ripe Stilton cheese), or medievalism – 'medieval mania', it called it – when in 1847 it pointed out that a history of a country may be recalled through its monuments. 'If by monuments are meant works of art, and if our history is to be read in those,' it wrote, 'we shall be treated by posterity as people who live in the Middle Ages, for everything around us partakes of the medieval character.'

So much for what the Revd H Wellesley wrote in the *Quarterly Review* in 1844: 'The century we live in is not more remarkable for its railways and marvels of science, than for a reaction from preceding barbarism in matters of taste'.

By 1870, the Early and High Victorian decades were over. Though the magazine settled down to mirror the prevailing more comfortable and worldly interests of its readership, it did not miss opportunities to remind them that much still needed to be done on the social front. In 1875, for example, when Prince Albert became head mason, 'Brother' Punch urged him to 'do your best to improve our public architecture; and, above all, the dwellings of the poor'.

Modernism, and contemporary foibles, in all their various guises, continued to be the butt of the sharp pencils of its cartoonists: the Arts and Crafts and Garden City movements; suburbanisation and its Tudorbethan cottages along new arterial roads; Cubist one-off houses of the wealthy; and American skyscrapers (the Empire State Building in New York, 1,480 feet high was, 'by English measurement ... no less than 15 chains, 3 poles, 2 yards and 2½ feet high', *Punch* recorded, or almost three times as high as the Great Pyramid, which it proceeded to illustrate by a cartoon of three Great Pyramids stacked on top of one another).

Throughout the two world wars publication continued, no doubt as a way of keeping up morale at home; but once peace had resumed it lost no time in drawing attention (literally!) to the shortcomings of politicians who had promised homes for the returning heroes; nor, indeed, to the importation of continental Europe's ideas on architecture, planning and development. The beautiful full-page line drawings of artists such as Bernard Partridge gradually gave way to a less formal, more whimsical style; and the elaborate, ponderous and often pedantic captions which were needed to explain, distil and fuse often complex associations of ideas gave way to a sentence or two.

The Second World War left a million buildings to repair and thousands of devastated acres to rebuild for a burgeoning population. *Punch* soon got to grips with austerity, materials and skilled labour shortages and the introduction of prefabricated building methods for the erection of Le Corbusian tower block prototypes.

The Festival of Britain buildings on the South Bank, a century after the Crystal Palace, were a foretaste of the New Jerusalem, with Skylon and the Dome of Discovery featuring often in its pages. When the *Architectural Review* deplored the despoilation of town and countryside alike in its special Outrage and Counter-Attack issues in the 1950s, *Punch* responded with its own Casebook of good and bad examples of planning, 'in which the paramount requirements of the kiddies, doggies, old folk and cripples have been kept continuously uppermost'.

The architects *Punch* most loved to lampoon were, not surprisingly, Corb, Sir Basil Spence (over his financial control of the building of Coventry Cathedral) and Richard Seifert who, in 1973, delivered the spoof Seifert Memorial Lecture, on the history of demolition, in the Reading Room of the British Museum, 'which is so very soon to be involved in the exciting Bloomsbury Redevelopment Scheme. You will all find yellow helmets under your seats.' More recently the target has been Richard Rogers.

Its cartoons were never more effective than when used in conjunction with comic verse. By 1959 the device was used for architecture, as in the Anti-Uglies (opposite the Foreword), and this verse from New Brickbats and Bouquets:

> An Atomic Power Station need not
> be entirely unlovesome, God Wot,
> if it soars like a lark
> from a National Park
> with a chimney by GILES GILBERT SCOTT.

With the Prince of Wales's intervention in the great architectural, planning and development debate of the latter part of this century, the professions finally lost

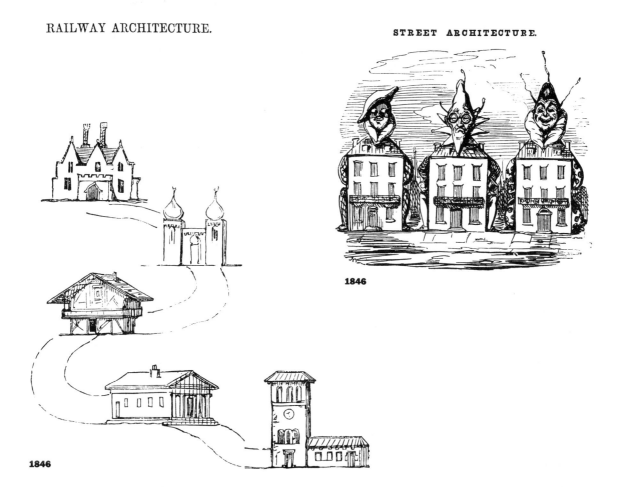

RAILWAY ARCHITECTURE.

STREET ARCHITECTURE.

1846

1846

any vestiges of mystique as far as *Punch* was concerned. And as a stylistic free-for-all ensued (reminiscent of the closing years of the nineteenth century) – Hi-Tech, Post-Modern, Romantic Pragmatism, Classical Revival – and conservationists won innumerable battles, the public rallied to the Royal cry to 'start a new Renaissance in Britain'.

Thumbing through 150 years of *Punch* we can see how right Kipling was when he wrote: 'How very little, since things were made, Things have altered in the building trade'. More than a few Pecksniffs are still discernible in the industry; and another Royal Prince is doing his best to emulate the great Albert's vision of building a better world for those in the inner cities and one which is more visually appealing to public taste.

The sought-after 'Renaissance' may still be a little way off. But then as Mr Punch and his battalions of cartoonists down fifteen decades have proved, where there's an earnest quest there's also a legitimate jest!

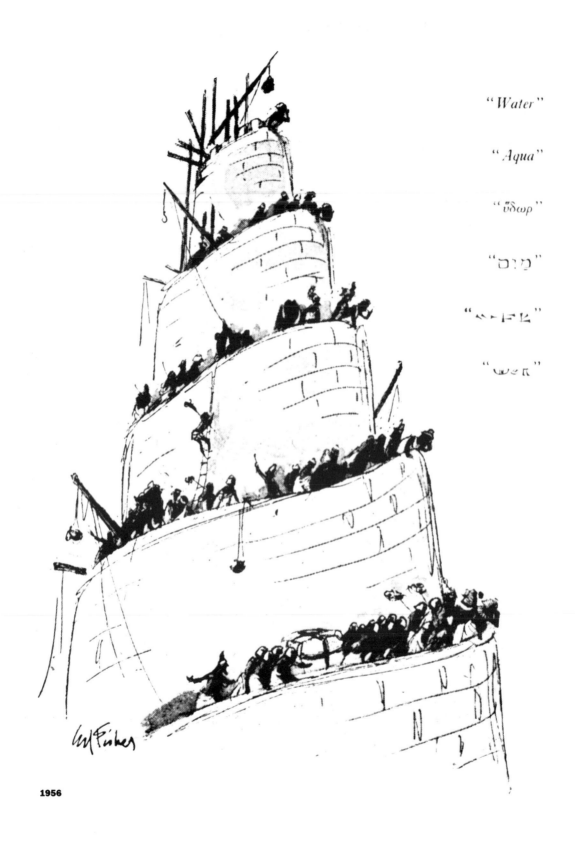

"Water"

"Aqua"

"ὕδωρ"

"מים"

"вода"

"水"

1956

THE PRESENCE OF THE PAST

A hardy perennial among cartoonists depicting architectural subjects is the historical antecedent for current developments, whether the Tower of Babel, the Walls of Jericho, the Great Pyramids of Giza or Bill Tidy's interpretation of how the druids awarded the contract for the erection of Stonehenge – on design rather than cost. Ah, those were the days.

In 1899, *Punch* accurately predicted how the monument on Salisbury Plain might be 'popularised' should it ever one day be acquired on behalf of the nation; while its possible use as a prehistoric greyhound-racing track was mooted in 1927 – the year after the first greyhound stadium opened at Belle Vue, Manchester.

Classical Rome was another common source of inspiration: from complaints about the architect not living in his own design but vacating it for his villa in the country, to Mark Antony looking for the 'naughty bits' recording his antics with Cleopatra on a triumphal arch.

But while Rome wasn't built in a day, as the saying goes, who could imagine the medieval master mason of one of our great cathedrals telling his client, the bishop: 'I'm afraid we couldn't undertake to deliver one in under three centuries'.

Cartoonist's licence often takes precedence over historical accuracy; but the force of many of the best examples relies on unlikely juxtaposition: the spiv brick salesman doing a deal on the Great Wall of China is one such case; using a builder's hoist as a passenger lift in the Middle Ages is another. As all students of elevators know, the first installation was in Louis XV's private apartments in Versailles which he used to gain access to his mistress, Mme de Chateauroux, on the floor below. Otis's steam-powered safety elevator was not demonstrated for another century.

Tourism, the mass-market activity unknown before the early years of this century, was a boon, especially when it contrasted so diametrically in its purpose and practitioners with its cultivated forebears on their Grand Tour.

A certain snobbery is all too prevalent in *Punch*'s depiction of the breed since it relied for its sales on the burgeoning middle classes. Snooks were cocked at those who lacked refinement or a classical education – particularly Americans and the working class. 'Say, we don't want to waste time here,' says the American to his colleagues arrived at a cathedral. 'Two of us can do the inside and the others the outside.'

The sensible, educated and slightly retiring (Brit), on the other hand, would marvel at the Acropolis and state: 'No, I wouldn't call them ruins. I prefer not to make value judgements'!

"The Borough Council Engineer says the top ten storeys must come down—some nonsense about controls."

1948

" . . . and that's jazz!"

1975

COMPETITION FOR THE DESIGN OF THE GREAT PYRAMID. THE JUDGES DISCUSSING THE RELATIVE MERITS OF THE COMPETITORS' WORK.

1909

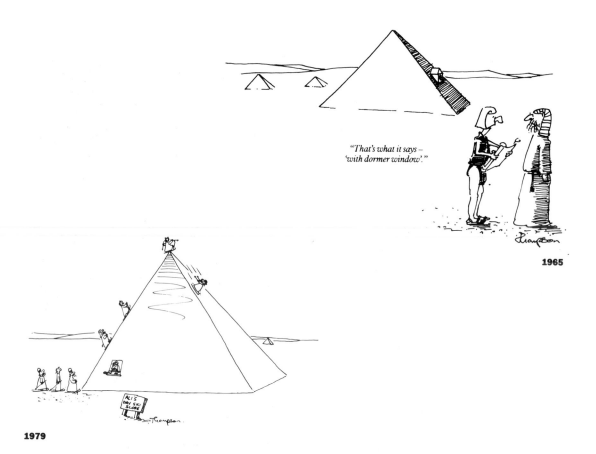

"That's what it says –
'with dormer window'."

1965

1979

"I see Shabatakhta finally grabbed the tomb-lining contract."

1969

20

"Must it stay just there? It ruins the view."

1949

1979

1955

"Go and tell the Chief Druid we were vandalised last night!"

1980

"I just live for the day when we catch those Roman bastards at it, that's all."

1982

The One. "WHY NOT GREYHOUND RACING?"
The Other. "THAT'S AN IDEA."

1927

HOW STONEHENGE MIGHT BE POPULARISED IF THE GOVERNMENT BOUGHT IT. SUGGESTION GRATIS.

1899

"*. . . and you can bet your life the architect lives in a nice little villa in the country.*"

1976

"*Where's the rude bit about me and Cleopatra?*"

1985

"These hill towns would be completely cut off if it weren't for the telephone."

1951

That very young Architect, Fadly (who believes in nothing of later date than the Thirteenth Century), invents a Gothic Hat!

1861

THE DAWN OF THE ELEVATOR.

The Lady Ermyntrude (aside). "IN SOOTH I KNOW MY LORD HATH CONTRIVED THIS FOR MY GREATER COMFORT, BUT, GOD WOT, RATHER WOULD I CLIMB THE STAIRS TO REACH MY BOWER ANY TIME!"

1929

"A cathedral? I'm afraid we couldn't undertake to deliver one in under three centuries."

1947

"Would you kindly settle an argument—is this, or is it not, the longest nave in Britain?"

1951

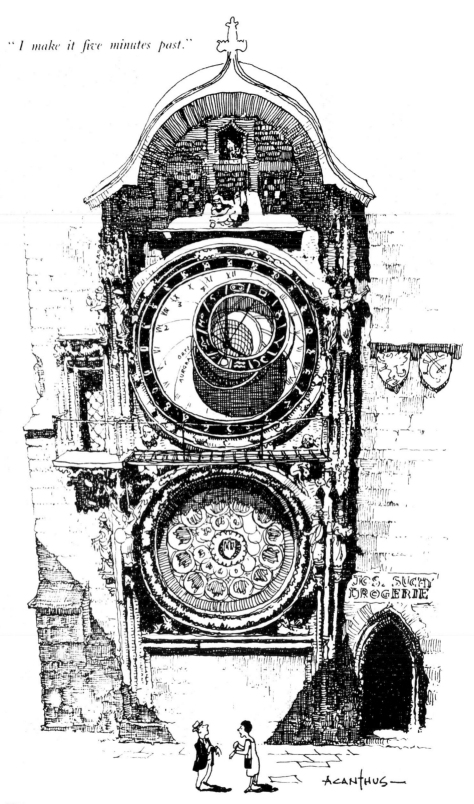

"I make it five minutes past."

1954

"You've got the Sistine Chapel job, Leonardo—they want you to design Michelangelo's scaffolding."

1982

"I won't be sorry when somebody gets this perspective problem sorted out."

1982

American Tourist (visiting Cathedral). "Say, we don't want to waste time here. Two of us can do the inside and the others the outside."

1924

"You and your 'All roads lead to Rome'!"

1950

"Somehow I never quite visualised it like this."

1972

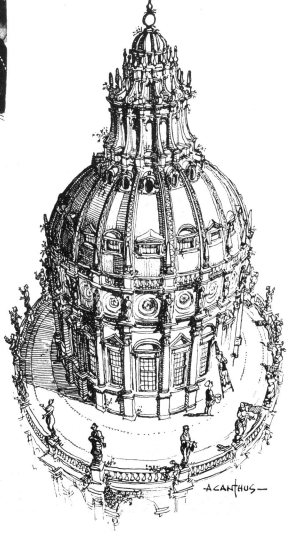

"Blowed if I can remember where I started."

1952

Profiteer Tourist. "I'LL GO AND SEE ANY BUILDINGS THAT HAVE ROOFS ON 'EM, BUT AS TO THE REST I SAY LET BYGONES BE BYGONES."

1923

"He says it sounds a really great idea and he thinks he knows where he can lay his hands on some bricks."

1988

HONEY-MOONING IN ITALY.

Fair American Bride. "OH, JOHN! TO THINK THAT PERHAPS VIRGINIUS STABBED HIS DAUGHTER ON THIS VERY SPOT, AND THAT JUST OVER THERE TULLIA DROVE OVER HER POOR FATHER'S DEAD BODY!"

John. "AH—VERY SAD—VERY SAD, INDEED! BUT, SAY, MATILDA, I GUESS WE'D BETTER LET BYGONES *BE* BYGONES. AND NOW LET'S GO AND HAVE A LOOK AT THE NEW POST-OFFICE."

1891

"No, I wouldn't call them ruins.
I prefer not to make value judgments."

1982

VIEWING THE ELGIN MARBLES.
" WHAT'S THAT, FATHER? "
" ER—ONE O' THEM ANCIENT BRITON JIG-SAW PUZZLES."

1934

"We were very impressed with the Acropolis."

1975

The Profiteer's Lady (in Rome). "WOT WAS THE COLISEUM, 'ENRY? A CINEMA?"

1921

LONDON

A GREATLY OVER-RATED PLACE

OUR VILLAGE SIGN.

1920

METROPOLITAN LIFE

Punch has always had an ambivalent attitude to the capital, safeguarding the interests of what it considers sacrosanct and castigating what it abhors. Originally, it was very much the metropolitan magazine; indeed, its original title was *Punch, or the London Charivari*. For the uninitiated the word *charivari*, first recorded in 1735, is of obscure origin but means 'a serenade of rough music, made with kettle, pans, tea trays, etc, used in France, in derision of incongruous marriages, etc, hence a babel of noise'.

As the modern city took shape, nothing was spared: the movement of monuments such as Temple Bar (it clogged the flow of traffic in Fleet Street, traditional boundary between the cities of Westminster and London); the 'improvement' of the Albert Hall by placing the Albert Memorial at its summit; roadworks in the Strand; new designs for the National Gallery (shades of a famous speech about 'monstrous carbuncles' here, but almost a century earlier); and the opening of Tower Bridge in 1894.

What it was most passionate in defending was St Paul's Cathedral, and rightly so. It campaigned against the threat of the railway bridge at Ludgate Circus (and lost, although the bridge's recent demolition will be welcomed).It campaigned against the threat of aerial advertising ('sky-signs of the times'). And it supported appeals for the restoration of the cathedral's stonework, ravaged by acrid London smog.

Controversial plans for new development at Paternoster Square after the wartime Blitz (again, shades of a famous Luftwaffe speech delivered at the Mansion House much later) prompted Acanthus, the pen-name of an architect-cartoonist, to suggest that the problem could be solved very simply, by replicating Wren's masterpiece on neighbouring sites surrounding the original, as a power station, offices, flats, car park and anything else which might be required, *ad infinitum*!

The only rival to St Paul's in Mr Punch's affections was the Crystal Palace, so named by him in 1850. The name stuck, which is hardly surprising given the official alternative for Joseph Paxton's brilliant invention – The Great Exhibition of the Works of Industry of All Nations – and how appropriate a description it was. His greatest sorrow was its destruction, by fire, at Sydenham in 1936.

Skylon, at the Festival of Britain exhibition on the South Bank, in 1951, the imagined threat of a digitised liquid crystal display face on Big Ben clock tower, and what Richard Rogers, the architect of the latest Lloyd's of London building in the City, might get up to elsewhere in the capital (given half a chance) gave full rein to the cartoonists' inventiveness.

REMOVAL OF TEMPLE BAR TO WESTMINSTER.

NOVEMBER 9, 1876.

An opportunity that ought not to have been missed.

1876

M. P. "DID YOU SEE THIS ADMIRABLE SUGGESTION IN THE PAPER, TO PULL DOWN THE TEMPLE BAR?"

Swell. "PULL DOWN THE TEMPLE BAR! A MOST EARNESTLY HOPE NOT—WHY, GOOD GWACIOUS! IT'S THE PWINCIPAL BARWIER BETWEEN US AND THE HORWID CITY!"

1852

38

METROPOLITAN PRIZE PUZZLES. No. 8.

THE BILLINGSGATE MARKET PUZZLE. (*Problem* 1.) HOW TO GET INTO THE MARKET. (*Problem* 2.) HOW TO GET OUT OF THE MARKET. (*Problem* 3.) HOW TO FIND YOUR WAY WESTWARD. (*Problem* 4.) HOW TO GET RID OF THIS OBSTRUCTION.

1883

THE BROWNS HAVE NOT YET BEEN ABLE TO GO TO SWITZERLAND THIS YEAR, BUT IT'S NEARLY AS GOOD GETTING TO A THEATRE NOW THAT THE STRAND IS "UP."

1898

OUR UNTRUSTWORTHY ARTIST IN LONDON.
IMPROVEMENT OF THE ALBERT HALL.
(Suggestion by Messrs. Guszard and Bunter.)

1907

A PROPOSAL.

'Arry 'Olborn (to Sally Strand). "DARLING! LET US BE UNITED."

Sally (blushing). "THIS IS SO SUDDEN! ASK PA—PA—PARLIAMENT!"

1899

THE REJECTED DESIGN FOR THE NEW LAW COURTS.

" One anonymous architect has sent in a frantic design, which the Commissioners have not chosen to exhibit."—Times, Feb. 11, 1867.

1867

MR. PUNCH'S DESIGNS FOR THE NEW NATIONAL GALLERY.

No. 1.—SUGAR-TONGS PATTERN.
NOT BY OWEN JONES.

No. 2.—STEARINE ORDER.
BORROWED BY BRODRICK.

No. 3.—GOTHIC HORSE-SHOE STYLE.
A SUGGESTION FOR STREET.

No. 4.—CROQUET STYLE.
HOW DO YOU LIKE THIS FOR A DOME, MR. BARRY?

No. 5.—THE TELESCOPIC STYLE,
OR HOW TO GET "TOP LIGHTS" FOR PICTURES, MR. DIGBY WYATT,
IF YOU PLEASE.

No. 6.—THE BOTTLE AND GLASS,
OR CONVIVIAL PERIOD—WHICH MIGHT HAVE HAPPENED IF BANKS HAD
DINED WITH BARRY.

1867

OUR GIANT CAUSEWAY.

(Opening of the new Tower Bridge, Saturday, June the 30th, by H.R.H. the Prince of Wales.)

Father Thames. "WELL, I'M BLOWED! THIS QUITE GETS OVER *ME!*"

1894

Country Farmer (seeing marvels of Metropolis). "DANG IT— THAT REMINDS ME! I COOM AWAY 'S MORNIN' AND LEFT OLD PIG-STY GATE OPEN."

1927

THE MAKERS OF LONDON.
SIR HANS SLOANE DESIGNS A SQUARE.

1912

1890   PICTURESQUE LONDON · OR, SKY-SIGNS OF THE TIMES.

Bernard Partridge

AMONG LIONS.

Trafalgar Square Lion (to St. Mark's Lion). "WE ALL SYMPATHISE WITH YOU IN YOUR LOSS. I ONLY WISH SOME OF OUR LONDON MONUMENTS WOULD COME DOWN AS EASILY!"

[The Campanile of St. Mark's fell Monday, July 14.]

1902

44

"Just think, my dear . . . if this is what man is capable of achieving in the seventeenth century, imagine what he'll be capable of by the twentieth!"

1973

ENLARGED AND (NOT) BEAUTIFIED.

WE furnish by anticipation a view of the new front of Buckingham Palace, with an additional suggestion of our own. The artist has been inspired apparently by a patriotic desire to assimilate the Palace of the Sovereign to the new shops of her subjects in the continuation of Oxford Street. It is a pity that this resemblance should be confined to the building. As the new front can hardly, by the wildest stretch of imagination, be deemed ornamental, why should it not be made useful? An agreeable addition to the Civil List might be obtained by letting out the ground-floor in shops, while HER MAJESTY and the Royal Family would be accommodated in the first floors, and the domestics in the attic story.

The Royal children might be allowed to acquire a practical familiarity with the retail commerce of the country, by taking a round of attendance in the shops successively, which would infallibly draw immense crowds to the establishments so favoured, and might be considered in the rents. A rush would certainly follow such an announcement as "Selling off.—The PRINCE OF WALES will serve out Groceries from 2 till 4;" or, "Try our Wellington Surtouts! Customers measured by PRINCE ALFRED, for this day only;" or, "The PRINCESS ROYAL and an immense lot of soiled Ribands." We cannot conceive any measure more likely to promote affability in the Royal children, and loyalty among the subjects of our gracious Sovereign.

1847

THE MAKERS OF LONDON.

Sɪʀ Cʜʀɪsᴛᴏᴘʜᴇʀ Wʀᴇɴ ᴘᴜᴛs ᴛʜᴇ ꜰɪɴɪsʜɪɴɢ-ᴛᴏᴜᴄʜ ᴛᴏ Sᴛ. Pᴀᴜʟ's.

1912

"ADVICE GRATIS."

Betsy Trotwood (Mrs. London City) to Mr. Dick (Mr. H-w-s). "Now ʜᴇʀᴇ ʏᴏᴜ sᴇᴇ Sɪʀ Cʜʀɪsᴛᴏᴘʜᴇʀ Wʀᴇɴ's Cʜɪʟᴅ, ᴀɴᴅ ᴛʜᴇ ǫᴜᴇsᴛɪᴏɴ I ᴘᴜᴛ ᴛᴏ ʏᴏᴜ ɪs, *Wʜᴀᴛ sʜᴀʟʟ I ᴅᴏ ᴡɪᴛʜ ʜɪᴍ?* Cᴏᴍᴇ, I ᴡᴀɴᴛ sᴏᴍᴇ ᴠᴇʀʏ sᴏᴜɴᴅ Aᴅᴠɪᴄᴇ."

Tʜᴇ ᴄᴏɴᴛᴇᴍᴘʟᴀᴛɪᴏɴ ᴏꜰ Oʟᴅ Sᴛ. Pᴀᴜʟ's sᴇᴇᴍᴇᴅ ᴛᴏ ɪɴsᴘɪʀᴇ ʜɪᴍ ᴡɪᴛʜ ᴀ sᴜᴅᴅᴇɴ ɪᴅᴇᴀ, ᴀɴᴅ ʜᴇ ʀᴇᴘʟɪᴇᴅ ʙʀɪsᴋʟʏ, "I sʜᴏᴜʟᴅ ᴡᴀsʜ ʜɪᴍ!"

"Mʀ. H-w-s," sᴀɪᴅ Mʀs. Lᴏɴᴅᴏɴ Cɪᴛʏ, "sᴇᴛs ᴜs ᴀʟʟ ʀɪɢʜᴛ. Wᴇ'ʟʟ ꜰɪʟʟ ᴛʜᴇ Fɪʀᴇ-ᴇɴɢɪɴᴇ ᴡɪᴛʜ sᴏᴀᴘ-ᴀɴᴅ-ᴡᴀᴛᴇʀ!"—"*David Copperfield,*" adapted.

1894

AN APPEAL TO THE NATION.

LONDON. "IF MONEY CAN SAVE THIS, SURELY IT WILL BE SAVED."

[Contributions to the St. Paul's Cathedral Preservation Fund should be sent to the Manager, *The Times*, Printing House Square, E.C.4.]

1925

Mr. Punch. "MAKE YOUR MIND EASY, SIR CHRISTOPHER, I'LL KEEP AN EYE ON IT."
["WREN never dreamt of the desperate attacks the sandy substratum would have to sustain."
Daily Paper.]

1901

THE HUMANITARIAN DEVELOPMENT OF ARCHITECTURE IN THE
AEROPLANING FUTURE.   A POSSIBLE USE FOR SUPERFLUOUS RUBBER.

1910

THE ARCHITECTS.
Nash (to Wren). "Don't talk to me about posterity. They keep propping you up and pulling me down."

1933

"Actually this is now very much as Wren intended us to see St. Paul's."

1941

1982

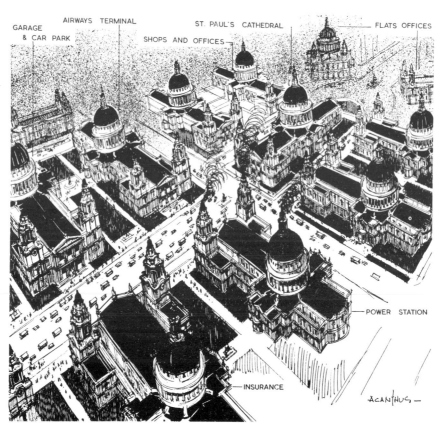

In view of the controversy concerning the development around St. Paul's the above solution is submitted in the hope of giving satisfaction to all.

1953

THE HAPPY FAMILY IN HYDE PARK.

1851

VIBRATION OF THE TUBE.
AWFUL EFFECT ON LONDON STATUES. AN ARTIST'S NIGHTMARE.

["Lord RAYLEIGH'S Committee is considering the vibration question."—*Daily Mail.*]
"Several new Tube Railways are projected."—*Daily Paper.*]

1901

SORROWS OF A SPONSOR

Mr. Punch. "AND TO THINK THAT IT WAS I THAT GAVE YOU YOUR NAME WHEN I WAS A MERE LAD!"

[In 1850, before the Great Exhibition began, Mr. Punch jokingly applied to the Crystal Palace the title which throughout its whole existence it continued to bear.]

1936

LIL OLD LONDON (ENG.).

SOME IMPRESSIONS INDELIBLY PRINTED ON THE MIND OF A CERTAIN VISITOR FROM THE U.S.A. OF A DAY'S CONDUCTED TOUR AROUND THE GREAT METROPOLIS.

OUR EUROPEAN TOUR SCHEDULE INCLUDED A MOST IMPRESSIVE DAY-TRIP AROUND LONDON'S HIGH SPOTS.

THE TOWER OF LONDON IS SURE SOME SKYSCRAPER—

THE HOUSES OF PARLIAMENT JUST TOO QUAINT—

CLEOPATRA'S COLUMN AND ST. PAUL'S REAL MAJESTIC—

WHILST, BELIEVE ME, THE CRYSTAL PALACE—

WESTMINSTER ABBEY—

WATERLOO BRIDGE—

AND WINDSOR CASTLE ARE THE LIL OLD CAT'S PYJAMAS.

WE SAW THE BALL GAME AT EARL'S CRICKET COURT—

AND PEEKED AT THE SMART SET AT THE ETON-AND-HENLEY POLO RACES.

BUT I'LL TELL THE WORLD THAT THOSE CUTE BEEFEATERS ON WATCH—

AT ROYAL VICTORIA PALACE WERE A THRILL THAT WILL NEVER FADE OUT.

1926

NO VISIBLE MEANS OF SUPPORT
"What do you mean—symbolic?"
(The Vertical Feature for the South Bank Exhibition is now under construction.)

1951

"*Of course we shall put it back after the Festival is over.*"

"*I just don't think it looks so dignified.*"

1951

54

1978

PUNCH
PLANS
FOR
PICCADILLY

Some fresh thoughts on rebuilding the Hub of the Empire

1. (above) The Classic

2. (right) The Mediaeval

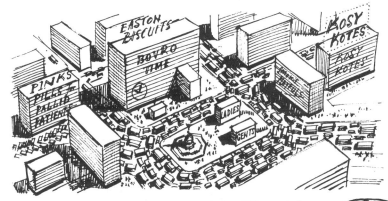

3. The Contemporary

4. The Four-Leaf Clover (for luck)

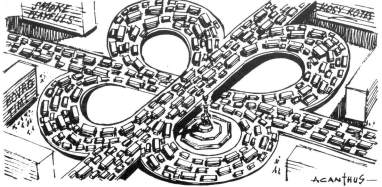

1959

DEADEYE DICK

Since he changed the Paris skyline with his design for the Pompidou Centre, Richard Rogers has been trying to do the same to London—**MAHOOD** illustrates his latest ideas.

POST OFFICE
TOWER HOUSING
DEVELOPMENT

BIG BEN
TV CENTRE

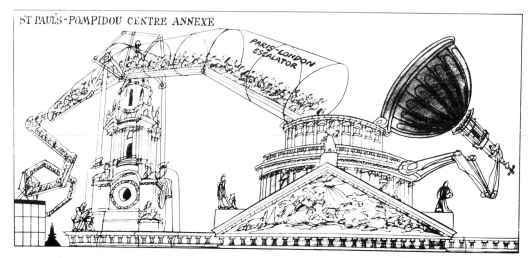

ST PAULS - POMPIDOU CENTRE ANNEXE

PARIS - LONDON
ESCALATOR

1980

TRAFALGAR SQUARE
FLYOVER AND OFFICE
DEVELOPMENT

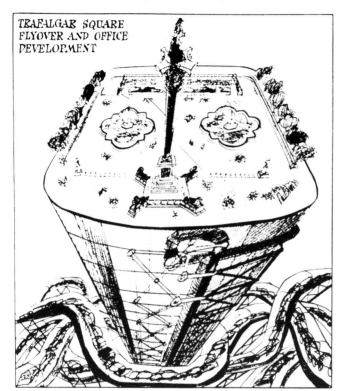

NATWEST TOWER
CITY WEATHER
PROTECTION

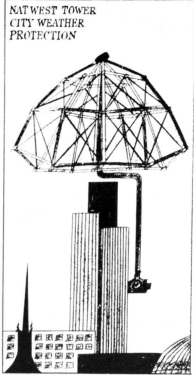

TOWER
BRIDGE
SHOPPING
CENTRE

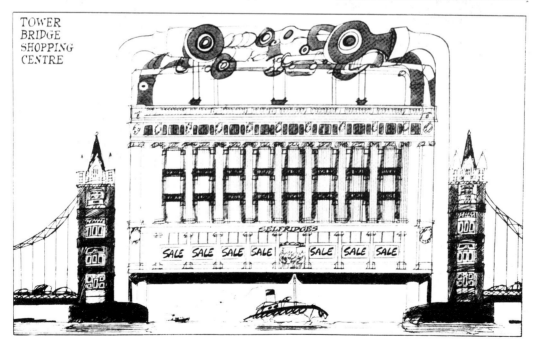

1980

"If the Leisure Park's successful they're going to convert coal mines and steel works next."

1984

T.DERRICK

ARCHITECTURE: of THE TERMITE STATE

1934

"And before you know they've slammed up another of these modern monstrosities."

1931

OUR GREEN AND PLEASANT LAND

By 1851 half the population of Britain was urbanised. London's population grew dramatically through the nineteenth century: in 1811 it was just over one million; by 1851 it was almost 2.4 million; by 1881, almost 3.5 million; and by 1901 more than 4.5 million. It remained the world's largest city until overtaken by Tokyo in 1957.

All this led to huge pressures to create a proper infrastructure, to build housing, roads and sewers. But due no doubt to the somewhat perverse character of the British, no sooner had people moved to the towns and cities than they wanted to escape – firstly to the suburbs, then to their rural roots. In 1946, Stevenage was designated the first post-war New Town, an alternative to both town and country which was meant to provide the best of both worlds.

Mass migration was made possible by the development of the railways from around the middle of the nineteenth century and, by the turn of the century, by the London Underground. Buses and motor-cars soon provided additional means for more people to get from A to B and back again, especially daily commuters, on newly-built roads, by-passes and later motorways. Weekend cottages became the ideal home away from home, even though villages were not immune from development, the loss of amenities or the penalties of two-car families. Between 1986 and 1990 the number of personal vehicles on the road in Britain actually increased by two-and-a-half million!

How could we possibly preserve what was – is – left? One suggestion, mooted by the American journalist and author, Tom Wolfe, not so long ago was that Britain should simply become one huge Disneyland-style theme park. But half a century earlier Thomas Derrick had already drawn that vision for *Punch*.

Perhaps, as Acanthus depicted in 1951, primitive Anglo-Saxons had evolved in a thousand years from living in beehive huts, via various elegant periods of architecture, to living in beehive tower blocks. But then progress takes its toll in so many ways, and how easy it is to destroy the things we love, including our environment.

When the neutron bomb was much in the news (before *glasnost* and the end of the Cold War) *Punch* showed two survivors of nuclear holocaust discussing a quaint half-timbered cottage, still left standing amidst the rubble: 'It was their one concession to the conservationists,' says one. 'The bomb destroys everything but listed buildings.'

While we can still enjoy what is left of our 'green and pleasant land' the cartoonist also helps us to laugh at ourselves. As the two pike-bearing soldiers prepare to defend the battlements from another attack, the one says to the other: 'Here they come again – doesn't the National Trust *ever* give up?' Thankfully not.

WHY NOT LIVE IN THE COUNTRY?

WHEN MR. SMITH LIVED CLOSE TO TOWN HE FOUND THAT THE VERY GENTLEST OF TROTS ENABLED HIM TO CATCH THE 8.40——

BUT NOW THAT HE IS LIVING IN THE COUNTRY——

HE HAS TO DO THIS——

AND THIS ——

AND THIS——

AND AGAIN THIS——

IF HE WANTS TO MAKE SURE

OF CATCHING THE 7.30.

1919

1914.—MR. WILLIAM SMITH ANSWERS THE CALL TO PRESERVE HIS NATIVE SOIL INVIOLATE.

1919.—MR. WILLIAM SMITH COMES BACK AGAIN, TO SEE HOW WELL HE HAS DONE IT.

1919

"WHERE EVERY PROSPECT PLEASES . . . ."

The Poster-Demon. "THAT'S A NICE VIEW. LET'S SPOIL IT."

[A Bill is now before Parliament to control the activities of the above fiend.]

1923

ONE ADVANTAGE ABOUT THESE ABSOLUTELY REMOTE COUNTRY COT-
TAGES IS THAT YOU CAN WEAR OUT SOME OF THE COSTUMES IN WHICH
YOU WENT TO THE FANCY BALLS THIS SEASON.

1914

Villager on left (referring to new memorial stone). "PRETTY, AIN'T IT?"
Other Villager (an incurable pessimist). "AH, SO 'TIS. BUT YOU MARK MY WORDS, MR. JUBBINS: THE FIRST EARTHQUAKE AS
HAPPENS ALONG, *DOWN SHE COMES!*"

1925

Lady from Chelsea to Villager (who is erecting new shed for her). "BUT, MR. PESCUD, COULDN'T YOU POSSIBLY MAKE IT LESS NEW LOOKING, YOU KNOW?"
Mr. Pescud (proud of his work). "WELL, LADY, THERE AIN'T NO DOUBT BUT WHAT IT DO MAKE TH' OLD COTTAGE LOOK A BIT SHABBY LIKE."

1923

THE BRITISH CHARACTER.
DETERMINATION NOT TO PRESERVE THE RURAL AMENITIES.

1936

THE PRESERVED AMENITY

1937

"... AND NOW YOU ARE GOING TO HEAR SID 'AMBONE SINGING 'TRIPE AND ONIONS.'"

1935

1954

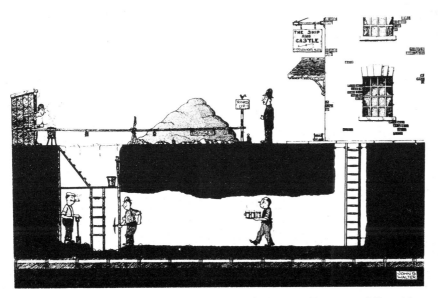

A POSSIBLE SOLUTION OF THE PERENNIAL HOLE--IN--THE--ROAD MYSTERY.

1935

Model Employer. "Now, Bates, I want you to ascertain the general opinion of the factory—geraniums or antirrhinums."

1937

THE BRITISH CHARACTER.
Predilection for week-end cottages.

1936

Shortsighted Old Dear (homeward bound). "CAN YOU TELL ME, YOUNG MAN, IF THIS IS THE EXCURSION BACK TO EALING BROADWAY?"

1924

PROGRESS.

SCENE I.—THE HIGH STREET.

SCENE II.—THE NEW BY-PASS.

SCENE III.—THE SAME AS SCENE II, ONE YEAR LATER.

SCENE IV—THE OLD HIGH STREET.

1932

THE LAST OF THE COUNTRYSIDE

1933

A HISTORY OF ENGLISH ARCHITECTURE

1951

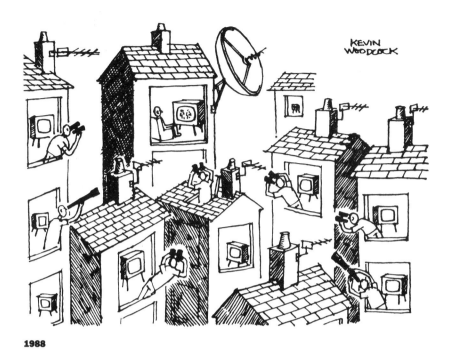

1988

The Dreaming Spires

1956

"*In its day it was probably thought quite impressive.*"

1952

*"Smash the next lamp on the left, flatten the pavement by the pub, nudge the sweet shop,
scrape the Market Cross, then just follow the skid marks to London."*

1979

1972   *"I'm a conservationist."*

*"Let's enjoy it while we can—this is where they're going to build
the new Leisure Centre."*

1983

"It was their one concession to the conservationists. The bomb destroys everything but listed buildings."

1983

"We're converting it into a four-small-church-complex."

1984

SELF-PRESERVATION

1938

"Here they come again—doesn't the National Trust ever give up?"

1981

79

"*I can remember the place before it was unspoilt.*'

1972

"*It'll be a heavenly place for us to retire to—whenever my wife gets stroppy.*"

1971

"On a clear day you can see
Prince Charles fuming."

1988

INCONVENIENCE OF UNIFORM ARCHITECTURE IN LONDON TERRACES.

GRIGSBY (A SHY BUT AMIABLE MAN) IS INVITED TO A SMALL JUVENILE PARTY AT NO. 47 (HIS BROTHER-IN-LAW'S), WHERE HE IS HELD IN GREAT FAVOUR BY THE CHILDREN, WHOM HE ALWAYS MANAGES TO STARTLE WITH SOME NEW AND AGREEABLE SURPRISE.

BY MISTAKE HE KNOCKS AT NO. 48, WHERE HE IS A COMPLETE STRANGER, AND BIDDING THE ASTONISHED MENIALS NOT TO ANNOUNCE HIM, HE RUSHES UP-STAIRS TO THE DRAWING-ROOM, WHICH HE ENTERS IN THE ABOVE EXTRAORDINARY FASHION!

[*The company assembled for Dinner at No. 48 are already much put out by the unconscionable lateness of an important guest.*

1875

DES. RES.

A burgeoning population, the scarcity of building land, and the shortage of skilled labour ensured that housing was a major focus of attention especially after the two world wars. The seriousness of the subject increased, rather than lessened, *Punch*'s instinctive reforming zeal, campaigning streak and satirical pose.

Homes 'fit for heroes to live in', the political promise of 1918, failed to materialise quickly; the same occurred in the wake of the Second World War. In the period between 1890 and 1914 only 14,000 homes were built: 600 a year. But the Housing and Town Planning Act of 1919 imposed a statutory duty on all local authorities to build with the help of government subsidy.

Much of the housing that resulted was low-density for the middle classes; the slum dwellers had to wait for higher-density blocks of flats and maisonettes until the mid-1930s. Even so, between the wars four million homes were built, largely taking the form of a pared-down version of the Garden City cottage.

But between 1934 and 1954 the population of Britain grew by a further 10 million, stretching resources and manpower to the limit as a result of the post-Second World War baby boom. Prefabrication of components, assembled on site using largely unskilled labour and tower cranes, was the solution. High-rise towers marched across areas of flattened terrace housing and green-field sites until the partial collapse of Ronan Point, in a gas explosion in 1968, combined with popular distaste for high-rise living, brought about their demise.

The magazine commented on the lack of identity of rows of similar dwellings and supposed breach of design copyright between architects; on the comparatively small size of rooms for those used to something grander; on the role of estate agents in marketing the des. res., a profession which was rarely seen in a favourable light; and the idiosyncratic design tastes of clients and their architects for the still-common 'one-off'.

The semi and suburbia inspired many quips: the 'borrowing season' for garden equipment; the 'semi-detachment' enjoyed by neighbours who insisted on painting the two halfs of a shared statue different colours; the desire to disguise monotonous ribbon development by erecting hoardings depicting the countryside. *Punch* also pointed out the contrasts between publicly and privately developed estates.

More recent concerns have been gentrification; dealing with powerful tenants' associations; the influx of house-buyers from the Middle East; home 'improvements', such as the pretentious stick-on porches in Moorish, Mr Pickwick or Ronchamp styles; and the difficulty – not long ago – of gaining a mortgage, even though the high streets are lined with building society branches.

AN EYE FOR ESSENTIALS.

Mamma (House-hunting for the Season). "IT'S A GOOD HOUSE FOR A DANCE, EMILY!"
Emily. "THE ROOMS ARE RATHER SMALL, AREN'T THEY?"
Mamma (who knows how Matches are made). "YES; BUT WHAT A CAPITAL *STAIRCASE!*"

1886

HOUSE-AGENT DEMONSTRATING TO PROSPECTIVE CLIENTS THAT THE VILLA IS WITHIN A
STONE'S THROW OF THE RAILWAY STATION.

1908

DES. RES.

(It is proposed that architecture shall enjoy copyright.)

Architect of Pomona Villas—West side (to Architect of Laburnum Villas—East side).
"HERE, YOU SCOUNDREL, YOU'RE INFRINGING MY COPYRIGHT!"

1901

ARCHITECTURE OF THE FUTURE.

The Architect. "IT'S A SPLENDID QUALITY OF STONE I'VE EMPLOYED FOR YOUR HOUSE—LASTS FOR EVER, AND GROWS A BEAUTIFUL COLOUR WITH AGE. OF COURSE IT'S HIDEOUS WHEN IT'S NEW."

The Squire. "AND HOW LONG WILL IT BE BEFORE IT GROWS A BEAUTIFUL COLOUR?"

The Architect. "WELL, YOU CAN HARDLY EXPECT IT TO LOOK DECENT IN *YOUR* LIFETIME!"

1889

THE COUNTRY HOUSE.
(What Our Architect has to put up with.)

Fair Client. "I WANT IT TO BE NICE AND BARONIAL, QUEEN ANNE AND ELIZABETHAN, AND ALL THAT; KIND OF QUAINT AND NUREMBERGY, YOU KNOW—REGULAR OLD ENGLISH, WITH FRENCH WINDOWS OPENING TO THE LAWN, AND VENETIAN BLINDS, AND SORT OF SWISS BALCONIES, AND A LOGGIA. BUT I'M SURE *YOU* KNOW WHAT I MEAN!"

1890

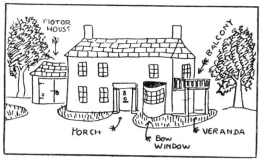

THIS IS THE ROUGH IDEA FOR HIS NEW HOUSE WHICH
MR. JONES GAVE TO HIS ARCHITECT.

AND THIS IS THE IDEA WHICH THE ARCHITECT THEN
GAVE TO MR. JONES.

1910

THE HOUSE-AGENT AT THE LATEST GARDEN CITY ADOPTS A COSTUME TO
HARMONISE WITH HIS SURROUNDINGS.

1912

House-hunter. "No, I don't think this would do. I doubt if there's a room in the house large enough to swing a cat in!"

Agent (to clerk). "Parkins, just step across to Miss Singleton's—number twenty-five—and borrow a cat; any average kind will do."

1912

GARDEN SUBURB IDYLLS.
The breadwinner's goodbye to his children.

1913

THE HOUSE-HUNTER; OR, THE AGENT WHO DID HIS BEST.

THE HOUSE-HUNTER; OR, THE AGENT WHO DID HIS BEST.

1921

THE MAN WHO ASKED A HOUSE-AGENT IF HE HAD A HOUSE TO LET.

1919

SINISTER SIGNS FROM SOUTH KENSINGTON.

Alarmed House Agent. "MADAM, WHAT HAVE YOU DONE TO MY PARTNER?"
Client. "I WAS JUST GIVING PARTICULARS OF MY FLAT, WHICH I AM ANXIOUS TO LET, AND WHEN I SAID, 'NO PREMIUM REQUIRED,' HE CRUMPLED UP AS IF HE'D BEEN SHOT."

1920

OUR DISTRICT AUCTIONEERS AND ESTATE AGENTS' ASSOCIATION'S
ANNUAL OUTING.

1925

Estate Agent. "BY THE WAY, THERE ARE SOME ROMAN REMAINS AT THE SOUTH END OF THE PROPERTY."

Buyer. "OH, IS THERE? WELL, SEE THAT YOU 'AVE 'EM CLEARED AWAY BEFORE I TAKE POSSESSION."

1926

SEMI-DETACHED.

"OH, DEAR! I DO WISH THAT TIRESOME MAN NEXT DOOR WOULDN'T LEAN AGAINST HIS MANTELPIECE."

1927

WHAT THE BORROWING SEASON IN THE SUBURBS MUST LOOK LIKE IF OUR HUMORISTS ARE CORRECT.

1928

THOUGH THEY SHARE THE FRONT GARDEN THE SMITHS AND BROWNS JEALOUSLY PRESERVE THEIR SEMI-DETACHMENT.

1928

THE TRIUMPH OF MIND OVER MATTER.

ROBINSON'S HOUSE ACCORDING TO HIS FRIEND SKETCHLEY DUDD THE ARTIST—

LOOKS SOMETHING LIKE THIS.

TO THE ARCHITECT IT WAS OBVIOUSLY THIS—

IT LOOKS LIKE THIS TO THE PLUMBER—

THIS SNAP I TOOK LAST SUMMER WILL GIVE YOU AN IDEA WHAT IT *REALLY* LOOKS LIKE.

BUT ROBINSON HIMSELF ALWAYS IMAGINED IT LOOKED LIKE THIS.

1935

94

Visitor. "CAN YOU TELL ME WHERE SIR FREDERICK DORJAMBE, THE FAMOUS ARCHITECT, LIVES?"
Sir Frederick. "YOU ARE ADDRESSING HIM."

1930

THE DREADFUL MONOTONY OF YESTERDAY—

HAS NOW BEEN CORRECTED.

1930

"WE'VE PUT THE BLINKIN' FURNITURE IN 'MON REPOS' INSTEAD OF 'CHEZ NOUS.'"
"THAT'S O.K. UNSCREW THE NAME-PLATES AN' CHANGE 'EM RAHND."

1935

House-Agent. "A MOST DESIRABLE MAISONETTE, SIR."
Client. "AH! AND I SEE IT'S ALSO GOT A GARDENETTE AND A GARAGETTE."

1932

CANNOT RIBBON DEVELOPMENT BE DISGUISED?
Work for our Artists and Scene-painters.

1935

" YOU SEE, IT 'S LIKE THIS: AS SOON AS YOU START PAYING THE INTEREST ON THE MORTGAGE THAT YOU 'RE TAKING OUT ON THE BUILDING THAT I 'M GOING TO START BUILDING ON THE SECURITY OF THE LIFE INSURANCE THAT YOU 'RE TAKING OUT TO SECURE THE TITLE-DEEDS, THEN I CAN START BUILDING THE BUILDING TO CARRY THE MORTGAGE THAT YOU 'RE STARTING PAYING THE INTEREST ON."

1935

THE VISION OF THE SPECULATIVE BUILDER.

THE COUNTY COUNCIL SCHEME.

1936

HER IDEAL HOME?

PEACE. "THE DESIGN'S A LITTLE ODD, BUT I MUST SAY IT DOES LOOK FAIRLY BURGLAR-PROOF."

1935

DES. RES.

PROGRESS

1939

THE STATELY HOMES OF ENGLAND

["A sub-standard of accommodation will have to be accepted during the housing emergency."—*Mr. George Hicks, Joint Parliamentary Secretary to the Ministry of Works.*]

1945

1944

"IT GOES WITHOUT SAYING, GENTLEMEN, THAT THE ACTUAL BLOCK OF FLATS WILL BE LARGER AND BUILT WITH REAL BRICKS AND THINGS."

1938

THE HOUSING PROBLEM.

PEACE. "BUT I THOUGHT I WAS TO HAVE GOT INTO MY TEMPLE LONG AGO."
THE OLD ARCHITECT. "EXTREMELY SORRY, MADAM—CONSIDERABLE DIFFI-CULTIES IN THE BUILDING TRADE. HOPE MY SUCCESSOR HERE WILL HAVE BETTER LUCK."

1919

"Yes, I think you'll find the place pretty well just as you left it when we took it over."

1946

BRITANNIA IN WONDERLAND

"It was still very uncomfortable . . ."

1945

What colossal great rooms our forebears used to live in : ———

Even now that they're turned into maisonnettes, there's still a shade too much of them.

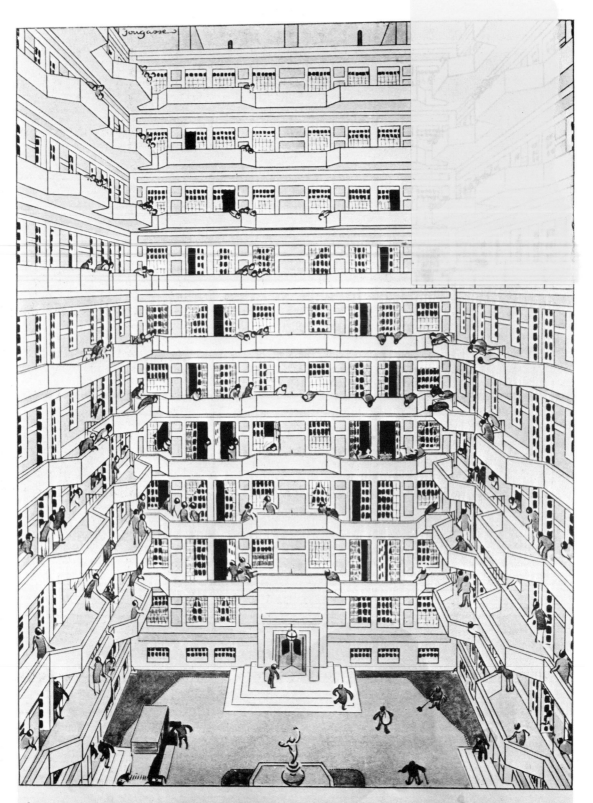

REMARKABLE OCCURRENCE IN THE HEART OF THE METROPOLIS. THE NEWCOMERS TO FLAT No. 21 USE THEIR BALCONY AS A BALCONY.

1932

THE DISTURBER OF THE PEACE

1948

FLAT-LIFE.
THE BIRD-BATH.

1936

" Yes? "

1939

1944

"I wondered why they were building these flats on stilts."

1953

"I understand they threw that one up specially, as a sop to the conservationists."

1973

"Door!"

1971

"A couple of passing Millwall fans got here before us."

1984

"They're detached of course."

1958

". . . and, as you can see, it's right bang in the Martini belt."

1964

"We've decided to put it on the market."

1977

*"But Mr Al Rashid, it's hardly **my** fault that the exchange of contracts is taking so long . . ."*

1977

"It probably won't make any difference, but I think you've left out a squiggle after that second curly thing."

1977

"For heaven's sake, Brian! Can't you forget for one minute that you're a chartered surveyor?"

1979

"Isn't that typical? I see the Joneses are starting to make a landing strip."

1963

"Mind? Good heavens, no, darling! In Kentish Town neighbours like that put £10,000 on the value of a house."

1981

HANDYMAN PUNCH

A pastel-tinted pebbledash or "Clinkerette" stone-look storm porch can banish ugly draughts and lend "Georgian" or "Moorish" character to your home, adding £££s to its value. Pre-moulded "Nylonene" accessories such as the stylish "Moggyflappe" pets' entrance or "Milkomayde" combination crate 'n' dial for empties are maintenance-free and give that finishing touch in a range of attractive styles from "Norman" to "Queen Anne" "South Pacific" door chimes are easily wired for extra charm.

Existing front doors, unless badly wormed or daubed by vandals etc., need not be removed before assembly of the storm porch. With knockers and locks routed out and the letterbox made good with proprietary filler, strip with wire wool and Rawlinson's No 2 Barnacle Remover or re-paint in gloss avocado to make a cosy feature of the inner vestibule. An elegant choice for the new outer door is the double-glazed "Mr Pickwick" in walnut-veneered sturdy blockboard with "bull's-eye" olde-worlde glazing.

For the modern town house or garden maisonette, builders' merchants also stock a large contemporary range, including the Scandinavian "Shirleen" and ultra-modern "Tracey" porch based on a design by Le Corbusier. Fitting is simp'icity itself with self-tapping clout hooks or an outdoor epoxy adhesive such as "Klam" but seal wintry weather out of ill-fitting seams with "Mastigunge" elasticised resin applied with a shiver's clasp-knife. Seek planning permission for loggias larger than 6.39m³.

1979

"Here you are, squire—genuine fifteenth-century, all mod cons, etc. Course, you haven't got a hope in hell of getting a mortgage."

1981

"I should decide quickly. It may be gone by tomorrow."

1972

1978

"You always find them around new developments. They're to keep the building inspectors away."

1983

"This is Shangri-la?"

1981

*"Of course, the challenge will be to restore it without **ruining** the satanic effect."*

1979

DES. RES.

"When you have finished here, James, the dining-room needs weeding."

1954

"Do let's buy it, Geoffrey."

1978

"They have a very strong Tenants' Association."

1978

JUST IN TIME."

Country Gentleman (who had been violently dragged into the road by his Wife). "GOOD GRA-
CIOUS, MY DEAR GAL, WH-WH-WHAT EVER'S THE MATTER?"

Wife (in terrified accents). "MATTER! LOOK WHAT IT SAYS ON THE BOARD OVER THERE—
AND WE WERE JUST UNDER THE HOUSE! HOW FORTUNATE I LOOKED UP! WE MIGHT 'A
BEEN—CRUSHED TO ATOMS!"

1881

BRAVE NEW WORLDS

The rapacious demands of development on land have not let up over 150 years. In 1892, *Punch* illustrated the 'Jerry-Building Jabberwock', a nonsensical beast based on Lewis Carroll's poem, who devoured all in its path, both buildings and landscape, to satisfy the needs of the new urban masses. Existing squares and other open spaces were equally under threat: in a Bernard Partridge cartoon of 1926 the speculative builder, pickaxe in hand, accosts a horrified Miss London: 'It's your lungs I want!'

New building types had to be accommodated. The cinema replaced the music hall as the most popular place of entertainment and, by 1932, just 25 years after the first was purpose-built, there were 250 in London, including the Trocadero at Elephant and Castle, seating 5,000. The corner shop was replaced by the supermarket, and new department stores, a cross between retailing palaces and museums, introduced new shopping patterns and modern alternatives to stairs – the 'moving staircase', which was like a conveyor belt, the escalator and the lift.

Demolition and rebuilding became a constant process as the pace of development increased. But woe betide the labourer who unearthed an archaeological remain in the path of a new office block: 'Start about here,' says the foreman, 'and the first man to find a Roman temple gets docked a quid . . .'.

After the Second World War the phenomenal increase in white-collar workers in the service sector fuelled the demand for offices and led to a succession of commercial property booms. Although at 600 ft the NatWest Tower is puny by comparison with its cousin skyscrapers in New York and Chicago, the size and quantity – as well as much of the quality – of new development was increasingly called into question, with The Prince of Wales leading the protagonists since his Hampton Court speech of 1984.

Architects, planners and developers have held their ground, for the most part. As Lowry (the cartoonist, not the painter) would have it, the 1st Battalion Estate Agents' Volunteer Rifles defend their position in the thick of battle, as they rally round their 'flag' which proclaims: 'This Valuable Plot For Sale'!

But the ultimate question remains – do property developers get to heaven? If so, even they might be in for a shock. Arriving at the pearly gates in his ethereal BMW, one is surprised to find his way impeded by a barrier and sign saying 'Please take ticket'. The supervisor informs him: 'National Car Parks took it over years ago!'

THE JERRY-BUILDING JABBERWOCK.

"BEWARE the Jabberwock, my son!
  The jaws that bite, the claws that catch!"—
Ah, CARROLL! it is not in fun
    Your song's light lilt we snatch.

Our Jabberwock 's a *real* brute,
  With mighty maw, and ruthless hand,
Who ravage makes beyond compute
    In Civic Blunderland.

Look at the ogre's hideous mouth !
  His tiger-teeth, his dragon-tail !
O'er Town, East, West, and North and South,
    He leaves his slimy trail.

And where he comes all Beauty dies,
  And where he halts all Greenery fades.
Pleasantness flies where'er he plies
    His gruesomest of trades.

He blights the field, he blasts the wood,
  With breath as fierce as prairie flame ;
And where sweet works of Nature stood,
    He leaves us —slums of shame.

The locust and the canker-worm
  Are not more ruinous than he.
"I 'll take this Eden—for a term ! "
    He cries, and howls with glee.

"Beauty? Mere bosh ! Charm? Utter rot !
  What boots your 'Earthly Paradise,'
Until 'tis made ' A Building Plot ' ?
    Then it indeed looks nice !

"O Jerry Street ! O Jerry Park !
  O Jerry Gardens, Jerry Square !—
You won't discover—what a lark !—
    One 'touch of Nature' there !

" 'This handsome Villa Residence' [walks ;
  Means mud-built walls and clay-clogged
And drains offensive to the sense,
    And swamps whence fever stalks.

1892

WANTED—AN OPEN-AIR MINISTER.

Speculative Builder (*to London*). "IT'S YOUR LUNGS I WANT!"

[Public protests are being made against the rumoured intention of converting the beautiful estate of the Foundling Hospital into a new Covent Garden Market or otherwise building over this fine open space and its adjacent squares.]

1926

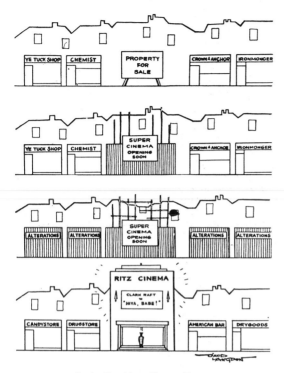

Little Chortlebury Goes to Town.

1946

IF YOU SHOULD SEE ANY LITTLE THING YOU WANT
IN THAT PET OLD CURIOSITY SHOP OF YOURS, BUY IT NOW.

TO-MORROW MAY BE TOO LATE. NEIGHBOUR-
HOODS CHANGE SO QUICKLY NOWADAYS.

1911

SMILKIN'S EMPORIUM.

Dear Sirs,—We are returning your design advertising our emporium, and will be glad if you will kindly instruct your artist to
delete the solitary giant in the foreground and put in a number
of people of the normal size.

We are, yours faithfully,

SMILKIN AND CO.

Block and Co.,
Colour Printers and Designers.

1925

SMILKIN'S EMPORIUM.

Dear Sirs,—We thank you for your amended design advertising
our emporium. It is now quite satisfactory. We return drawing
and will be glad if you will kindly push on printing.

We are, yours truly,

SMILKIN AND CO.

Block and Co.,
Colour Printers and Designers.

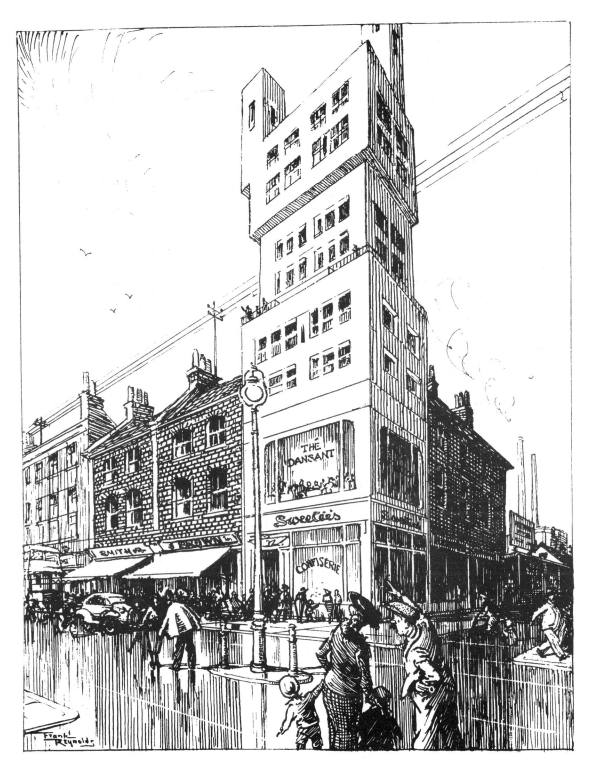

Former Resident. "STRUTH! THEY 'AVEN'T 'ALF REBUILT THE LITTLE SWEET-STUFF SHOP!"

1937

"CONFOUND THESE AUTOMATIC LIFTS!"

1937

ARCHITECTURE AS THE HANDMAID OF COMMERCE.
Shopwalker. "HAIRPINS, MADAM? CERTAINLY—THIS WAY."

1925

BRIGHTER LONDON.
SPEEDING UP THE ESCALATOR.

1925

"CHIC" CASTS ITS SPELL ALONG OUR HIGH STREET.

1933

1983

1956

1980

"Oi, you! Hop it!"

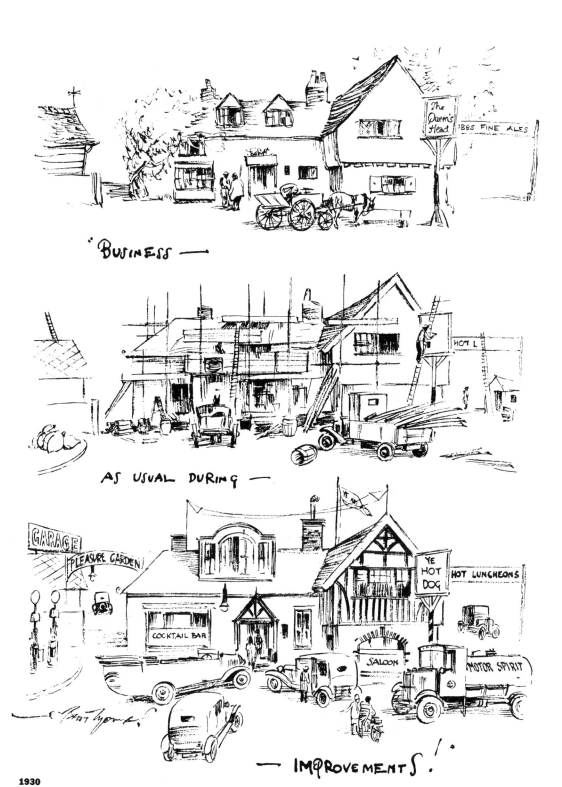

"BUSINESS —

AS USUAL DURING —

— IMPROVEMENTS!

1930

". . . AND WHEN I TOLD 'ER I SPENT MOST OF ME TIME KNOCKIN' ABOUT WEST-END 'OTELS AND PLACES SHE WOULDN'T BELIEVE ME."

1934

"Very few in the Club to-day, Watkins."

1940

"Not so loud, Albert. Remember walls have ears."

1939

". . . And then came the war."

1972

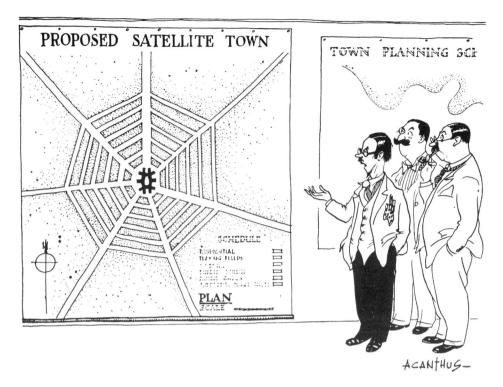

"Of course, the main idea is to attract people."

1946

1972

"And our New York office is just here on the 20th floor, directly facing the Empire State Building."

1939

Now the development charge has been abolished—

—let us hope some of our streets will lose that dreadful gap-toothed appearance.

1953

"He's a one-man business."

1973

NEW TOWNS FOR OLD

1946

"Start about here and the first man to find a Roman temple gets docked a quid . . ."

1954

1985

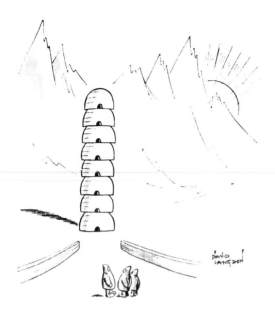

" THE PROVISION OF A LIFT WOULD NATURALLY PUT THE RENT UP."

1938

"There are a couple of conservationists on the selection panel, so you'd better bring the tree."

1971

"There must be some misunderstanding, the three and a half million was just for the model."

1971

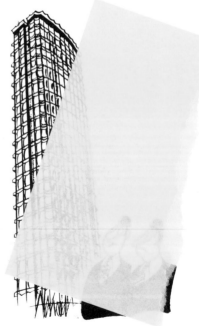

"I hear the Chancellor has plans to turn it into a hostel for bankrupt property speculators."

1974

"They say he was
a child prodigy."

1983

"I warned him not to let that property
developer in."

1974

"This is the wall, Foster. We'd like you to knock up some sort of apt and symbolic mural—you know the sort of thing—The Chairman and Board presiding over the Twin Spirits of Art and Industry as they rise from the Waters of Diligence to reap the rich harvest of Prosperity while the Three Muses, Faith, Hope and Charity flanked by Enterprise and Initiative, bless the Corporation and encourage the shareholders."

1979

"*You know what I'd like when I retire? A nice little office block by the sea.*"

1972

1980

1954

The Architect Explains

ARNOLD ROTH interviews various practitioners

"Of course, I've a profound respect for traditions, old boy—after all, without them, what have you got?"

". . . and, as a creative person, I feel it only right to assert my emotional self."

*"There is no such thing as what people **need**. I give them what they **want**."*

"It's no longer a matter of aesthetics—but one of economics."

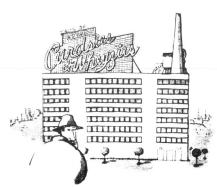

"I let my buildings speak for me."

1962

*"If people are mesmerised by the word 'Georgian,'
why should I disillusion them?"*

*"To me, it's more than a religious monument—it's
the expression of an ideal."*

*"I merely assert modern man's desire to reassume his
place in nature."*

*Man, in my opinion, is only human. I am helping him to
rediscover the human scale."*

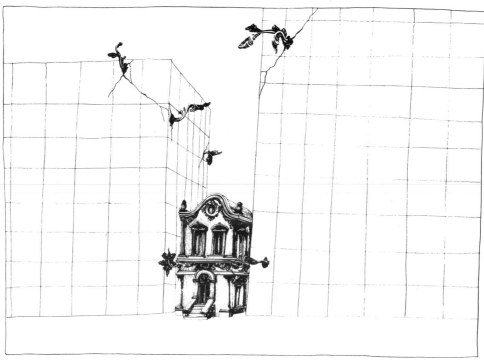

1973

"Thank God! I thought it was going to be another
of those damn soulless concrete boxes!"

1972

"National Car Parks took it over years ago!"

1978

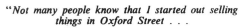

"Not many people know that I started out selling things in Oxford Street . . .

. . . Department stores, office buildings, blocks of flats . . ."

1970

"Of course, there's bound to be some initial opposition to our redevelopment scheme."

1973

"*I have a feeling this may not
be successful . . .*"

1971

1971

Architect's Wife. "You talk of your profession being overcrowded, Arnold, but here's your chance. Why not see the Town Clerk of this place about a reconstruction scheme?"

1934

"And here, a hundred feet below ground and blast-proof, the normal functions of local government will go on."

1980

"There's a large available workforce, and no shortage of caddies."

1987

"*We need a new image, Croftley. Design us one of London's best-loved landmarks.*"

1972

"*I don't want anything Prince Charles might object to. Then again, I don't want my heirs to be saddled with a listed building.*"

1987

UTILE CUM DULCE.

Inquisitive Gent. " YOU WILL—A—THINK' ME VERY INDISCREET—BUT I CAN-
NOT HELP WONDERING WHAT THIS ELABORATELY-CARVED AND CURIOUSLY-
RAMIFIED STRUCTURE IS FOR. IS IT FOR ORNAMENT ONLY, OR INTENDED TO
HEAT THE HOUSE, OR SOMETHING?"

Fastidious Host. " O, IT'S THE *DRAINS!* I LIKE TO HAVE 'EM WHERE I CAN
LOOK AFTER 'EM MYSELF. POOTY DESIGN, AIN'T IT? MAJOLICA, YOU KNOW. . .
HAVE SOME CHICKEN?"

1872

IN THE EYE OF THE BEHOLDER

Is 'beauty' in the eye of the beholder, or is it an absolute? The question has been frequently asked down the decades, never more so than now. Lord St John of Fawsley, chairman of the Royal Fine Art Commission, even raised it in a House of Lords debate not so long ago. Asked what he thought about the Pompidou Centre in Paris, designed by two Royal Gold Medallists for Architecture, Richard Rogers and Renzo Piano, Spike Milligan replied that the best thing about it was its location – Paris!

Yet in 1872 *Punch* showed an aesthete's glorification of plumbing not on the outside of a building, as at Pompidou and the new Lloyd's of London headquarters, but coming through his dining room. Not knowing what it is at first, the inquisitive dinner guest asks: 'Is it for Ornament only, or intended to heat the house, or something?'; to which his fastidious host replies: 'O, it's the drains! I like to have 'em where I can look after 'em myself. Pooty design, ain't it? Majolica, you know . . . have some chicken?'

The magazine enjoyed satirising new decorative trends. In 1903 the architect and designer M H Baillie Scott was shown reading a paper in 'The Home Made Beautiful According to the "Arts and Crafts",' – it features his own furniture and furnishings.

The British passion for nostalgia and mock-ness of any kind invited mockery, whether of the contrived interior of a 'real old English Inn', or the storm-damaged half-timbering to the exterior of a Tudorbethan cottage. Says the jobbing builder to the owners: 'Shall I peel orf what's stuck on, or shall I tack up what's blowed orf?'

Modern houses produced a reaction of a different kind. The fashionable, trousered lady, poised with a cigarette in a holder, challenges the visitors to her streamlined 1930s house: '*Do* tell me you *loathe* it'. And as the occupants of a concrete Cubist box enter the gate to their property, the neighbours comment: 'Well, anyway, the people who have taken it seem to be the usual shape!'

In challenging the Pecksniffs of the architectural, planning and development world, The Prince of Wales has decided to put his money where his mouth is – a latter-day Prince Albert, the greatest royal builder since Charles II.

While it is still too early to tell what will be the end result of his crusade to 'throw a proverbial brick through the inviting plate glass of pompous professional pride', he is already assured of public support and, more than likely, the backing of considerably more members of the development industry than care to be identified. 'Beauty' may be an abstract concept, but as Mel Calman's pocket cartoon character quipped, on behalf of us all: 'I don't know much about ART, but I know a carbuncle when I see one . . .'.

NATURE V. ART.

Æsthetic Friend. "YES, THIS ROOM'S RATHER NICE, ALL BUT THE WINDOW, WITH THESE LARGE BLANK PANES OF PLATE-GLASS! I SHOULD LIKE TO SEE SOME SORT OF PATTERN ON THEM—LITTLE SQUARES OR LOZENGES OR ARABESQUES——"

Philistine. "WELL, BUT THOSE LOVELY CHERRY BLOSSOMS, AND THE LAKE, AND THE DISTANT MOUNTAIN, AND THE BEAUTIFUL SUNSETS, AND THE PURPLE CLOUDS—ISN'T THAT PATTERN ENOUGH?"

1892

TO BRIGHTEN FOOTBALL.

(Appropriate designs for goal and costume of goal-keeper.)

"CORINTHIANS."

"VILLA."

"HOTSPUR."

1913

146

Country Cousin (after prolonged inspection of building operations).
"I don't see the sense of putting statues on the top of your buildings."

1925   *Friend.* "Statues? Those aren't statues—they're *bricklayers*."

THE LATEST STYLE OF ROOM DECORATION. THE HOME MADE BEAUTIFUL.
According to the " Arts and Crafts."

1903

1978

"I can't wait for the Bauhaus to arrive. I just don't have the face or the figure for all this Renaissance crap!"

American. "SO THIS IS A REAL OLD ENGLISH INN?"
Barmaid. "NO; BUT IT WILL BE IN A FORTNIGHT."

1928

AFTER THE GALE.
"AND WHAT ABOUT THIS 'ERE 'ARF TIMBERIN? SHALL I PEEL ORF WHAT'S STUCK ON, OR SHALL I TACK UP WHAT'S BLOWED ORF?"

1933

"OF COURSE, PERSONALLY, I WOULDN'T DO ANYTHING MORE TO IT."

1935

Mistress (in ultra-modern house). "WHAT HAVE YOU DONE TO YOUR HAND, GWENDOLEN?"
New Maid. "IF YOU PLEASE, MA'AM, I CAUGHT IT ON THE DINING-ROOM WALLPAPER."

1932

"DID I REALLY UNDERSTAND YOU, MISS WILSON, TO USE THE EXPRESSION, 'A COSY NOOK,' IN CONNECTION WITH THE HOUSE YOU WISH ME TO DESIGN FOR YOU?"

1936

Modernist (just returned from holiday). "AFTER ALL, ENID, THERE'S NO PLACE LIKE HOME."

1933

Owner. "Do TELL ME YOU *LOATHE* IT."

1936

"WELL, ANYWAY, THE PEOPLE WHO HAVE TAKEN IT SEEM TO BE THE USUAL SHAPE!"

1934

1979

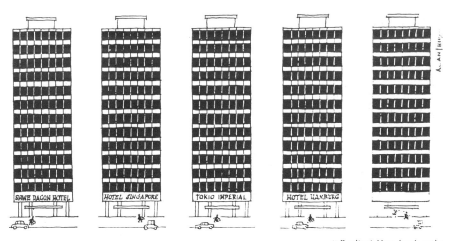

1968

1974

"I still prefer the Gothic."

1972

1966

"It looks like classicism is creeping back."

CHRONOLOGY OF EVENTS: 1841–1990

1841 *Punch, or the London Charivari* first published
Hong Kong acquired by Britain
The Reform Club opened

1842 Nelson's Column erected (Landseer's lions added 1867)
The Builder (latterly *Building*) launched

1843–44 Publication of *Martin Chuzzlewit*, by Charles Dickens, which introduced the character of Pecksniff, architect and land surveyor

1843 The first underwater pedestrian tunnel opened, Rotherhithe to Wapping

1845 The first park for Londoners opened, Victoria Park in the East End

1846 The first municipal museum opened, in Sunderland

1847 Foundation of the Institution of Mechanical Engineers
British Museum opened

1848 Temporary floodlighting of the National Gallery by electric arc-lamp
Palm House, Kew, opened
W. H. Smith and Son became the first multiple retailer

1849 The first co-educational school opened in Britain, at Liscard, Cheshire
Cholera epidemic a forerunner to the 'Great Stink' of 1858. By 1865, £4 million spent on an 83-mile-long sewerage system and measures stemming from various health acts

1851 The Great Exhibition in Hyde Park had six million visitors in five months
50.6 per cent of the British population now lived in towns
Marble Arch, designed by Nash, moved from Buckingham Palace to Hyde Park

1852 New Palace of Westminster formally opened
The first public lavatories opened in Fleet Street
The first free public lending library opened, Manchester
The first working-man's club opened at Clare Market, London

1853–56 Crimean War

1856 Bessemer process permitted mass-production of steel
Victoria and Albert Museum opened

1857 Clock Tower (Big Ben) built at the Palace of Westminster
Completion of British Museum Reading Room

1858 Royal Opera House, Covent Garden, completed

1859 Foundation of the Central Association of Master Builders

1860 New Palace of Westminster completed

1863 The first underground railway opened, the four-mile Metropolitan Line between Paddington and Farringdon Street
The forerunner of the first modern department store in Britain opened by William Whitely, in Bayswater
The first rented poster sites in Britain, in Leeds

1864–70 Victoria Embankment built, reclaiming 37 acres from the Thames

1864 Science Museum opened
The first Peabody Building in Commercial Street, Spitalfields

1867 The first commemorative plaque placed by the Royal Society of Arts on Byron's House, off Cavendish Square
Reinforced concrete patented by Joseph Monier, Paris

1868 Foundation of the Surveyors' Institute, formerly the Surveyors' Club (founded 1792, later the RICS, 1946)
First office block with an elevator (lift), New York

1869 The first municipal housing completed in Liverpool

1871 Foundation of the Institution of Electrical Engineers
The first school built by a local educational authority in Britain, at St Austell, Cornwall
Royal Albert Hall opened

1872 The first reinforced concrete building, at Greenwich, Connecticut, USA

1874–82 Royal Courts of Justice built

1874 The first sighting of double-glazing, at Cranfield Court, Bedfordshire

1875 The first cabman's shelter, in Acacia Road, St John's Wood
Albert Memorial completed
First plans for Bedford Park

1877–86 Shaftesbury Avenue built

1877 The first purpose-built department store, Bon Marché, Brixton
The first aluminium manufactured in Britain, at Oldbury, near Birmingham
The first permanent concrete bridge opened, at Seaton, Devon

1878 Permanent electric lighting at Victoria Embankment
Edison and Swan produced the first successful incandescent electric light
The first factory lit by electricity in Britain, at Stanton Ironworks, Derby
Temple Bar, the historic boundary between Westminster and the City, demolished and rebuilt ten years later at Theobald Park, Cheshunt
Cleopatra's needle, c.3,400 years old, erected on the Embankment

1879 Prudential Assurance Company building, Holborn (and 1899)

1880 Trial lengths of the Channel Tunnel dug from both Britain and France, then abandoned
Natural History Museum opened
Pre-stressed concrete introduced by P. H. Jackson, San Francisco

1881 The first electric power station for both public and domestic use, at Godalming, Surrey
Blueprints introduced by Marion and Co, London

1884–9 Savoy Hotel built

1885 The first steel-framed building by William Le Baron Jenney, Chicago

1887 Queen Victoria's Golden Jubilee celebrations

1888 County councils set up, including the LCC to govern the 117 square miles of London, except the City
Working-class dwellings built with bathrooms, Port Sunlight, Cheshire

1889 The first electric elevator (lift) installed in Britain, by Otis at Crystal Palace
The first mosque in Britain built, at Woking, Surrey

1890 Forth Bridge opened
The first Tube with electric trains in deep-level tunnels opened (Northern Line)

1894 Tower Bridge opened
The Penny Bazaar, Manchester, opened by Michael Marks and Tom Spencer, as the first variety chain store

1895–1903 Westminster Cathedral built

1895 The first National Trust property, a four-and-a-half acre nature reserve at Barmouth

1896 The first British cinema, at 2 Piccadilly Mansions
The first modern Olympic Games, Athens
The first National Trust building: The Priest's House, Alfriston, Sussex
The first steel-framed building in Britain: Robinson's Emporium, West Hartlepool

1897 Tate Gallery opened
The first motor-car service station, or garage, opened in Brighton

1898 The first escalator, or 'moving staircase', in Britain installed at Harrods
Miss Ethel Mary Charles became the first woman to qualify as an architect
The first car park in Britain, at a non-motoring event, Henley Regatta
The first reinforced concrete, multi-storey building in Britain: Weaver's Mill, Swansea

1899–1902 Boer War

1899 Howard's *Garden Cities of Tomorrow* introduced the modern concept of town planning
The first purpose-built motor-car garage, Southport

1901–13 The Mall laid out: Admiralty Arch, Queen Victoria Memorial, and Buckingham Palace east front remodelled

1901 Accession of King Edward VII
The first electric tram in London, from Hammersmith to Kew
The first multi-storey car park, off Piccadilly Circus
The first building erected from prefabricated concrete sections: cottage built at Cobbs Quarry, Everton

1903 The first LCC Commemorative plaque on Holly Lodge, Kensington, house of Lord Macaulay

1904 The first block of flats built from prefabricated concrete sections, Eldon Street, Liverpool

1905 Kingsway opened, between Strand and Holborn

1906 The first family holiday camp, at Caister-on-Sea, Norfolk

1907 The first purpose-built cinema in Britain, the Balham Empire
Imperial College opened

1908 The first outdoor telephone kiosks, probably in Nottingham

1909 Selfridges, Oxford Street, opened
The first swimming-pool with mixed bathing in Britain, at Holborn Baths

1910 Accession of King George V
London Palladium built, one of 60 large halls for variety and music-hall entertainment

1912–21 King George V Dock, Port of London, built

1912 The first concrete road in Britain, at Saltney, Cheshire

1913 The first p[...]de of neon lighting in
Britain, at [...] West End Cinema,
Coventry S[...], London

1914–18 World W[ar I]

1914 Foundatio[n of the Town Planning]
Institute

1915 The first air ra[id on London, by]
Zeppelin, destroyed [...] Ro]ad,
Stoke Newington
The Archit[ectural Association] Air Raid
Section be[came the first in] Civil
Defence u[nit in Britain]

1918 Women gr[anted the right to vote]

1919 Bauhaus sch[ool of design founded] by
Gropius at We[imar, Germany]
The first housing [subsidies paid to]
builders and loca[l authorities in Bri]tain

1922 Foundation of the Institution of
Structural Engineers

1923 The first piped music in Britain, at the
Ideal Home Exhibition, Olympia
The first by-pass in Britain, at Eltham

1924 Liberty's, Regent Street, completed

1926 General Strike
The first greyhound-racing stadium, at
Belle Vue, Manchester

1928 The first PABX telephone exchange in
Britain, at Liverpool Street Station

1929 London Transport Headquarters, by
Charles Holden

1931 British Commonwealth of Nations
formed
Shell-Mex House, Embankment,
completed
The first concrete lamp-standards in
Britain, in Liverpool

1932 Broadcasting House, Portland Place,
completed

1933 County Hall completed
Battersea Power Station completed

1934 Senate House, London University,
completed

1935 Green Belt designated around London
Trocadero Cinema, Elephant and Castle
completed (5,000 seats)

1936 Accession, and abdication, of King
Edward VIII
Accession of King George VI
The first regular public television
transmission
The Crystal Palace, re-erected in
Sydenham after the Great Exhibition,
burnt to the ground
Peter Jones, Sloane Square, completed
Demolition of the Adam brothers'
Adelphi

1937 Foundation of the National House
Builders' Registration Council
Dolphin Square, Pimlico, the largest self-
contained block of flats in Europe,
completed
Five-day working week introduced in
Britain, by Marconi Co. and Alfred Bird
Co.

1938 Finsbury Health Centre completed
Foundation of the Institute of Quantity
Surveyors

1939–45 World War II
Blitz bombings destroyed a third of the
City of London and much of the docks

1939 The first Anderson Shelters erected by
residents of Islington

1941 Foundation of The Federation of Master
Builders

1944 Education Act created free secondary
education for all

1945 Last air raid on the City, left a total of 164
acres in ruins, and 10 Wren churches
destroyed
The first fluorescent lighting in Britain, at
Piccadilly Circus Underground Station;
street lighting followed in 1946, in Rugby
and London

1946 Stevenage designated the first New
Town

1947 Town and Country Planning Acts passed

1948–49 The 'Berlin Airlift'

1948 Britain accepted US aid through the
Marshall Plan for post-war
reconstruction
Establishment of the National Health
Service
The first full-size supermarket in Britain
opened at Manor Park, London

1949 The first self-service launderette in
Britain opened in Queensway, London
The first closed-circuit television system
installed on a permanent basis, at Guy's
Hospital

1950–53 Korean War

1950 Peak District designated the first National
Park in Britain

1951 The Festival of Britain opened by King
George VI from the steps of St Paul's
Cathedral; on the South Bank, 27 acres of
new buildings erected, including the
permanent Festival Hall, and temporary
Dome of Discovery and Skylon

1952 Accession of Queen Elizabeth II
Britain's first atomic weapon exploded

1953 E P Hillary and Sherpa Tenzing reached the summit of Everest
Coronation of Queen Elizabeth II

1954 Roger Bannister ran the first mile in under four minutes

1955 The City of London became a 'smokeless zone'

1956 Queen Elizabeth II laid the foundation stone for the new Coventry Cathedral
Britain's first atomic power station opened at Calder Hall
Sir William Holford's proposal for Paternoster Square, St Paul's
Gower Peninsula, Wales, designated the first Area of Outstanding Natural Beauty

1957 The Suez Crisis

1958 The first motorway opened in Britain, Preston by-pass section of the M6
The first parking meters in Britain installed by Westminster City Council

1959–82 Barbican redeveloped as a residential and arts complex

1959 Route 11 (now London Wall) linked Moorgate and Aldersgate Street

1960 The first urban motorway in Britain: M62 Stretford-Eccles by-pass

1961 The first betting shops opened
Guildford Cathedral consecrated
The first self-service petrol filling-station in Britain, Southwark Bridge

1963 Hilton Hotel, Park Lane, altered the London skyline, followed by London Telecom Tower (1966), Centre Point (1967) and Hyde Park Barracks (1970)
Letraset introduced

1967 Civic Amenities Act created conservation areas
North Sea gas first piped ashore

1969 Neil Armstrong became the first man on the Moon

1971 London Bridge transported to Lake Havasu, Arizona and reassembled in the desert as a tourist attraction
The first busway: 12-mile bus-only route, Runcorn, Cheshire

1973 Britain entered the Common Market

1974 Covent Garden market moved to Nine Elms. Market buildings saved by local action

1975 Oil first pumped ashore from the North Sea
Channel Tunnel cancelled for the second time

Acknowledgement: Many of the innovations in this Chronology were taken from *The Shell Book of Firsts*, by Patrick Robertson, Ebury Press and Michael Joseph, 1974

1976 The first supersonic transatlantic passenger service began with Concorde
National Theatre and Museum of London opened

1977 Queen Elizabeth II's Silver Jubilee

1979 Election of Mrs Margaret Thatcher as Britain's first woman prime minister

1981 Wedding of The Prince and Princess of Wales watched by an estimated television audience of 750 million worldwide
London Docklands Development Corporation established
NatWest Tower (600ft) opened

1982 Falklands War
Thames Barrier completed

1984 The Prince of Wales decried 'monstrous carbuncles' in his speech to the RIBA's 150th anniversary celebrations, at Hampton Court Palace

1985 Live Aid charity concerts reached the largest ever television audience worldwide: 1,500 million people in 160 countries
Broadgate redevelopment began in the City of London

1986 'Big Bang' deregulation of the Stock Exchange
Lloyds headquarters, architect Richard Rogers, opened
The Prince of Wales called for a 'new Renaissance' in Britain

1987 The Prince of Wales delivered his 'Luftwaffe speech' at the Mansion House

1989 The Prince of Wales unveiled plans for a model development on his Duchy of Cornwall estate at Poundbury, outside Dorchester
The Prince of Wales published his book, *A Vision of Britain*, which was also turned into an exhibition at the V&A and a television documentary

1990 The Prince of Wales addressed the American Institute of Architects, Washington DC
Norman Foster, architect of the Hongkong and Shanghai Bank headquarters, Hong Kong, knighted
The Prince of Wales's Summer School in Civil Architecture, Oxford and Rome
Duchy of Cornwall submitted planning application for Poundbury development, Dorchester

INDEX OF CARTOONISTS

"Oh no!"

1987

1971